A sociology of
special education

By the same author
Educational Subnormality

A sociology of special education

Sally Tomlinson
University of Lancaster

Routledge & Kegan Paul
London, Boston and Henley

First published in 1982
by Routledge & Kegan Paul Ltd
39 Store Street,
London WC1E 7DD,
9 Park Street,
Boston, Mass. 02108, USA and
Broadway House,
Newtown Road,
Henley-on-Thames,
Oxon RG9 1EN

Set in 10/12 Baskerville by
Inforum Ltd, Portsmouth
and printed in Great Britain by
Billing & Sons Ltd
Guildford, London, Oxford and Worcester

Library of Congress Cataloging in Publication Data

Tomlinson, Sally.
A sociology of special education.
Bibliography: p. 186
Includes index.
1. Handicapped children — Education.
2. Educational sociology.   1. Title.
LC4019.T65   371.9   81-12118
                        AACR2

ISBN 0-7100-0940-2
ISBN 0-7100-9003 X (pbk.)

Contents

Acknowledgments

This book is a product of my continuing sociological interest in special education, sustained throughout the 1970s in a study of *Educational Subnormality* (Routledge & Kegan Paul, 1981) and in the production of a set of readings on *Special Education: Policy Practices and Social Issues* with Len Barton (Harper & Row, 1981).

I would particularly like to thank Len Barton, Michael Barrett, Janet Finch and John Reynolds for their comments on draft chapters of this book, and their helpful comments and discussion on issues in special education, which we are all only just beginning to grapple with.

I would also like to thank my husband and children for their sceptical comments and for caring about my work.

To preserve confidentiality concerning individuals and schools quoted in case studies in this book, all names and sometimes sex of respondents have been changed and information has been rearranged to prevent possible identification.

Introduction

This book aims to widen debates about special education by introducing sociological perspectives: asking questions about the social structures and social relationships that occur when part of a mass education system in an industrial society develops as 'special' rather than normal, about the conflicts between individuals and groups that arise in special education, and about the beliefs and ideologies used to justify actions and relationships in this type of education. Current dominant perspectives on special education can variously be described as medical, psychological, administrative and educational, particularly prescriptive-educational. There has been a functional sociological tradition in special education, exemplified by the use of social surveys to discover 'how many' handicapped children or children with special needs there are, but by and large, theory and practice in special education are not informed by sociological perspectives.

Given current hostility to sociology as an academic activity, some might argue that there is no need to develop a sociology of special education, but discussions with professionals and practitioners involved in special education, with students preparing for both special and normal teaching, with parents of handicapped children and with sociological colleagues persuades me that there is scope for beginning to develop sociological perspectives on the activities that make up 'special' education. To claim this is not to deny the legitimacy of other views and perspectives, or the tremendous importance of the activities of all those engaged in special education, but it does appear that state special education, just over a hundred years old in Britain, is attempting to cope with dilemmas and conduct debates that might well, at this point in time, be illuminated by sociological perspectives. It does seem that some professionals and students are beginning to find the 'recipe' knowledge – pedagogical, clinical, psychological – which is offered to them dissatisfying in that they are often asked to accept as unproblematic what are, in fact, very debatable notions and concepts. There *is* a need to acquire wider social, historical and political perspectives on the policies, practices and processes which make up special education. It is hoped that the book will be of interest to students preparing for both special and normal teaching, to practitioners, professionals and administrators engaged in special education and perhaps to parents of children who have been designated in post-1978 terminology, as having 'special needs'.

Although much illustrative material in the book refers to the majority of children in special education, those in what are described in chapter 3 as the 'non-normative' categories, for example, mild educational subnormality, slow learners, maladjusted or disruptive, it is hoped that practitioners dealing with the minority of children in special education, the 'normative' categories of blind, deaf, physical handicap etc., will also be interested.

. It is also hoped that sociologists will be interested in the book, as to date they have shown remarkably little concern about special education. Even those working full-time in the area of the sociology of education seem to have accepted without much comment the progressive removal of more and more children from the normal education system into special education, until in the last quarter of the twentieth century we have a situation where it is proposed that 20 per cent of the school population will require some form of special education at some time during their school career (*Special Educational Needs . . .*, 1978). Sociologists of education particularly can no longer afford to ignore the 'special' education of a fifth of all school-children.

The first chapter of the book attempts a justification of the need for a sociology of special education by pointing out existing and new sociological perspectives and their relevance. Chapter 2 examines the social origins and development of special education from the early nineteenth century, noting that education systems and their parts do not develop out of purely humanitarian motives, but out of prevailing dominant social and economic and professional vested interests.

Chapter 3 examines some of the crucial dilemmas in special

education which, although usually presented in educational terms, reflect wider social and political conflicts and interests. The problem of who is selected for special education and the accompanying rhetoric of 'special needs' is examined, and the dilemmas of egalitarianism which have contributed to the 'integration' debate are noted. Chapter 4 examines the professionals who legitimate the removal of children into special education and notes the expansion in the number of professional people who now have vested interests in discovering more and more children in need of special education. This chapter draws on a study of the assessment of children for ESN-M schools to illustrate the conflicts, rather than the 'smooth teamwork', which characterise professional activity in special education.

Chapter 5 briefly reviews the position of parents, pupils and teachers in special education. Despite the rhetoric of parental involvement, parents are often associated with incompetency and are inadequately involved; pupils are associated with negative attributes – *in*capacity, *in*ability and powerlessness; teachers are seen to have more power and be less accountable than their colleagues in normal schools, but still to be subject to a variety of constraints. Chapter 6 examines what has been called the 'deserted garden' of the special school curriculum (Williams, 1980) in the light of current calls for greater accountability. The chapter discusses the aims of special schooling, with particular reference to the curriculum for 'slow learners', and questions why the special school curriculum has so far escaped much scrutiny. Chapter 7 comprises a discussion of ethnic minority children in special education with particular emphasis on the issue of the 'over-placement' of children of West Indian origin in ESN-M schools, remedial education, and behavioural units. The treatment of minority group children can raise questions about the whole nature of special education and help clarify its function and purposes.

Finally, chapter 8 discusses the possible future of special education in the light of new legislation and changing ideologies. It is suggested that special education may become very important as a means of removing children who are 'troublesome', in the widest possible sense, from normal education, despite an ideology of 'integration'. The children will be legitimated as unemployable, or as, at best, semi- or unskilled labour. A new tripartite system may develop, comprising independent education, comprehensive education and special education. Special education will be functional for social order, since those who have received a special education may be subject to more direction and control.

Although, in this book, the terminology of disability, defect and statutory or descriptive categories of handicap are used, these labels are regarded as social constructions developed in particular historical contexts – they do not necessarily have any intrinsic meaning. Changing terminology in special education – often a source of confusion – is related to its social and political functions and development. The emphasis in the book is on understanding special education as a social process in a social context.

Chapter One · Why a sociology of special education?

In Britain, the way in which children are categorised out of ordinary or mainsteam education and into special education is generally regarded as enlightened and advanced, and an instance of the obligation placed upon civilised society to care for its weaker members. Special education is permeated by an ideology of benevolent humanitarianism, which provides a moral framework within which professionals and practitioners work.

But it is important to recognise that the recognition, classification, provision for, or treatment of, children who have been at various times defined as defective, handicapped or as having special needs, may very well be enlightened and advanced, but it is also a social categorisation of weaker social groups.

All over the world, powerful social groups are in the process of categorising and classifying weaker social groups, and treating them unequally and differentially. The rationalisations and explanations which powerful groups offer for their actions differ from country to country and the ideologies supporting systems of categorisation differ. The notion that a variety of professional groups are solely engaged in 'doing good' to the children they refer, assess, place and teach in special education is something of a rationalisation. Professionals and practitioners have vested interests in the expansion and development of special education. They also have very real power to define and affect the lives and futures of the children they deal with. A crucial factor in special education is that, unlike other parts of the education system, the children concerned cannot speak for themselves, and despite the growth of parental pressure groups, parents still have little influence on special education processes. The clients of special education, children and their parents, have the least say and influence over what happens to them, and are subject to the most pressures, persuasions and coercion, of any group in the education system.

State special education is a sub-system of the wider normal education system.[1] It has developed to cater for children who are categorised out of the ordinary education offered to the majority of children in the society. It is important to stress at the outset that in modern industrial societies, which increasingly demand qualifications and credentials acquired through the education system, to be categorised out of 'normal' education represents the ultimate in non-achievement in terms of ordinary educational goals. Occupational success, social mobility, privilege and advancement are currently legitimated by the education system; those who receive a 'special' rather than an ordinary education are, by and large, excluded from these things. The rationale for exclusion has been that children were defective, handicapped or, more recently, have special needs. The result of exclusion is that the majority of the children are destined for a 'special' career and life-style in terms of employability and self-sufficiency.

Special education has been steadily increasing in size and importance over the past hundred years, and it often has appeared to be in a permanently dynamic state of change. But education systems and their parts do not develop spontaneously, they do not mysteriously adapt to social requirements, change without intent, and they do not necessarily develop in order to benefit different groups of children. Education systems, as Archer has pointed out (Archer, 1979), develop their characteristics because of the goals pursued by the people who control them and who have vested interests in their development. They change because of debates, arguments and power struggles. Changes in the form, organisation and provision of special education are not the result of mysterious processes of evolution, nor are they benevolent adaptations to new social requirements. Change happens because certain people want it to happen and can impose their views and goals on others. Thus, changes in the law relating to special education, in statutory categories, in separate or integrated provision, in increased professional involvement, in special curricula, and so on, occur as a result of deliberate decisions by people who have power to make the decisions.

Similarly, special education did not develop because individuals or groups were inspired by benevolent humanitarianism to 'do good' to certain children.

The idea that the development of special education was solely a matter of 'doing good' and was civilised progress, can possibly be traced to eighteenth-century humanism and nineteenth-century Christian reformism. But humanitarianism can itself become an ideology, legitimating principles of social control within a society. For example, A.F. Tredgold, who published an influential text-book on *Mental Deficiency* in 1908, dedicated his book to 'all those of sound mind who are interested in the welfare of their less fortunate fellow creatures'. But Tredgold also served on a com-mittee concerned with the sterilisation of defective people, and supported the idea of euthanasia for idiots and imbeciles.

The Charity Organisation Society, who took an interest in the defective and feeble-minded from the 1880s, urged social reform based on Christian principles of 'love, working through indi-vidual and social life' (Mowat, 1961). But they also urged that the feeble-minded be segregated in institutions and made to perform useful work.

This book attempts to bring sociological perspectives to bear upon those social processes, policies and practices which com-prise special education. The processes of special education are very complex, as are most social processes. Theory and practice in special education are informed by a variety of disciplines and approaches, but, by and large, sociology is not one of them. Medical, psychological, educational, administrative and technical approaches all influence and inform special education, but the sociological input is currently very limited. Sociological perspec-tives should be able to help all those concerned with special education by making clearer what is happening and why it is happening, particularly the way in which people or groups exer-cise power and influence, and can shape and change special education.

Tasks and values in sociology

A major task of sociology is to demystify social processes and social situations. John Rex wrote that: 'Sociology is a subject whose insights should be made available to the mass of people in order that they should use it to liberate themselves from the mystification of social reality that is continually provided by those in our society who exercise power and influence' (Rex, 1974, Preface).

Much of what happens in social life is the product of power struggles and vested interest, and special education is no exception. Each of the professional groups involved in referring, assessing, recognising, treating, teaching or administering in special education has its own vested interest, its own sphere of competence and a variety of powers. The people who are involved in special education are in the position to mystify others, particularly as special education is one of the most secret areas of education, in which 'confidential files' are the rule rather than the exception.

On a more general level, the task of sociology is to describe, analyse, explain and theorise about social interaction and social relationships. Sociology attempts to show that social reality can be studied from a variety of perspectives, that there are regularities which underlie the social structures and social process which people create and live within, and that there are social groups and movements which seek to account for, or legitimate change in these structures and institutions. Sociology cannot, of course, change social situations. This is the prerogative of the social participants themselves, who exercise practical, political and moral judgments. Special school teachers, for example, continually make judgments about the capabilities of the children they teach, often based on social rather than education criteria. The ideology of cultural disadvantage is often used to explain 'slow learners'.

'The poor achievements of many slow learners are due as much to the limitations of their cultural background as the limitations of ability' (Gulliford, 1969, p. 15). The assumption here is that teachers are unable to teach lower social class children adequately, because of cultural factors outside their control. Sociological perspectives might help teachers to question the value-assumption in this kind of statement, and change their practice accordingly. Only the teachers themselves are in a position to change what they actually do, but sociology could help them to recognise what they are doing. Sociology can make clear what the value-assumptions are of the people who are able to determine the life-chances of others and question the basis upon which decisions are made about other people. Sociology refuses to take for granted the explanations that people with power offer for their actions, or the official definitions of social situations. Sociological perspectives are important, and they should not go unrecognised or undeveloped any longer in the area of special education.

However, sociological intervention in special education will not necessarily be welcomed, and may even be regarded as unnecessary, or disturbing. An article which was mildly critical of the Warnock Committee on Special Educational Needs (1978) for accepting psychological perspectives rather uncritically and for failing to consider sociological perspectives (Lewis and Vulliamy, 1979) was condemned by a member of the Warnock Committee as 'hard and callous' (*The Times Educational Supplement*, 29 December 1979).

There is the possibility that sociological interventions in special education will be regarded as critical and threatening simply because they question the conventional perspectives, recipe knowledge and vested interests which are currently dominant in the area.

But if sociological perspectives have largely been lacking, sociologists, by their own lack of interests, have only themselves to blame. They were not represented on the Warnock Committee and are not consulted by those responsible for framing and changing the forms of special education. To date, sociologists have shown remarkably little interest in special education. Despite claims of objectivity, sociologists are often as much influenced in their choice of studies by prevailing ideologies as anyone else, and accept the treatment of certain social groups as 'natural' and therefore unworthy of study. Thus, over the past thirty years, sociologists have devoted much time and energy to demonstrating the inequities of selection by 'brightness' in education while ignoring the progressive removal of more and more children from normal education on the grounds of defect, dullness, handicap or special need.

It should be said that although sociologists can describe, analyse, theorise, clarify and demystify, they cannot do this in an objective way which assumes a value-freedom on their part, as some earlier sociologists had claimed. The debate on facts and values has a long history in sociology (Weber, 1949; Myrdal, 1944) and the consensus produced by the debate was that, while sociologists have no special claim, any more than natural or physical scientists, to impose their value-judgments on their analysis, they must make clear their own value-standpoint. This was articulated quite carefully by Kellman in 1970:

> We must recognise that social research, particularly on significant social issues, cannot be value-free, nor is there any reason why it should be. What is important is that we be actively aware of the values we bring to our own research, that we acknowledge them publicly and try in every way possible to take account of them in the formulation and execution of our own research and in the interpretation of our findings. (Kellman, 1970, p. 94)

If sociologists are going to research in, and theorise about, special education, they will have to make their own value-position clear, but equally, they will not be able to impose their judgments on others. For example, in a piece of research carried out in the mid-1970s (Tomlinson, 1981), the value-position taken was that to be categorised as mildly educationally subnormal, was more a legitimation of low social status than the treatment of an educational need. This position questioned the prevalent common-sense assumption that to be mildly mentally or educationally retarded is a prerogative of the lower social classes. It turned back-to-front the literature on ESN-M children which attempts to trace causal explanations for educational subnormality in low social class or cultural disadvantage (see, for example, Stein and Susser, 1960; Gulliford, 1969). It pointed out that categorising children as ESN-M may be more of a solution to a problem of social order than an aid to education. This kind of value-position may very well be unacceptable to some people involved in special education, but it is only by making their own position clear that sociologists will be able to be of any relevance and to join in current debates on change and development in special education.

Dominant perspectives on special education

During the nineteenth century, the medical profession developed and sustained an interest in all kinds of 'defect', and it was medical influence which dominated the commissions and committees on defective children in the late nineteenth and early twentieth centuries (Egerton Commission, 1889; Committee on Defective and Epileptic Children, 1898; *Report of the Royal Commission on the Care and Control of the Feeble-Minded*, 1908).

Clinical definitions of various types and grades of defect, and subnormality, became the prerogative of medical men. A medical superintendent at one of the first idiots' asylums devised a test for feeble-mindedness. It included looking for 'a v-shaped palate, large coarse outstanding ears, a fixed stare and a curved little finger' (Pritchard, 1963, p. 137). After the 1870 Elementary Education Act, which ushered in mass education, state educators recognised the more obvious handicaps of blindness and deafness and epilepsy and also began to define a problem of feeble-minded children in schools. Gradually, the notion developed that special, rather than ordinary, education should be offered to children who were, by definition, troublesome in the ordinary schools. This meant that educational administrators and the teaching profession developed an interest in defining defective but educable children. Special educators originally had some influence on decision-making for 'special instruction' – the head teacher of special schools for educable defective children was originally a member of the team who decided which children were defective, but generally teachers in the sub-system of special education had lower status than other teachers and only recently have they achieved more influence and parity with other teachers.[2]

The early twentieth century was a period when definitions of defect were consolidated and more special provision made, and this coincided with the development of the 'science' of psychology and the rise of the mental testing movement. Gradually, the new profession of psychology came to have a major influence in defining which children should receive a special education.

Esland has pointed out the way in which the cultural and political standpoint of psychologists has always been regarded as unproblematic, which meant that the judgments of psychologists appeared to be only 'technical diagnosis' (Esland, 1976, p. 261). In fact, psychologists often make judgments as much on the basis of their own social, cultural and political beliefs as on any objective 'science' (Tomlinson, 1981). In addition, both medical and psychological personnel have had vested career interests in special education since its inception, and the development of special education during the twentieth century can be viewed in terms of the vested interests of the professional groups, medical, psychological, educational and administrative, each anxious that their perspectives and influence should predominate, yet recognising a mutual interdependence. From the 1890s, the notion that it should be a 'team' decision as to which children should be recognised as candidates for special education has made it difficult to ignore any professional group in the assessment processes. The creation of ancillary professional groups has meant that there are a variety of other influences and perspectives on special education – social workers, psychiatrists, speech therapists, counsellors, careers officers, physiotherapists, education welfare officers, probation officers and health visitors are some of these groups; and all offer their own areas of 'knowledge' and have vested interests in the continued expansion of special education.

Technological developments in special education will also bring in more personnel, but they will be linked to existing perspectives. For example, neuro-surgical advance hopes to give simulated vision to the blind by implanting electrical devices:[2] this kind of development will be linked to medical interests. Practitioners' interests will be furthered, and new personnel with the requisite skills will be employed to use computers in special teaching programmes. The production of an individual learning programme (ILP) for every handicapped child became a legal requirement in the USA with the passing of Public Law 94–142 (Zettel, 1978), and this kind of provision could only be attempted with computer assistance.

However, the perspectives of disciplines such as medicine and psychology and the action of professionals and practitioners are themselves constrained by the structures of the society. The structure of industrial society has always provided a number of contradictions for those involved in special education to resolve. Until recently, the profit motive in such a society dictated that as many members as possible should be productive and even the defective or handicapped must work if possible. If not, contradictions arise as to how much of the society's resources should be allocated to the handicapped. Similarly, the preparation of a productive, educated work-force in ordinary schools was seen, after 1870, to be impeded by handicapped or defective children. A contradiction which has still not been resolved after a hundred years is the provision for, and control of, potentially 'troublesome' groups of children, while keeping the cost of provision low, but encouraging as many as possible to be eventually productive and self-sufficient.

Existing sociological perspectives on special education

There is, of course, an existing sociological tradition in special education, although many practitioners would not recognise it as such. This is what came to be called the structural-functionalist approach, epitomised by a concern for order, balance and equilibruim in a society (Parsons, 1952). The handicapped, in this approach, and also possibly in the popular consciousness, have become associated with the kind of deviance which Durkheim would have recognised; they are 'not normal' because of the definition of 'normality' applied by the rest of society (Hargreaves, 1979). The dominant concern within this approach has been the 'fitting in' of the handicapped, adults and children, into society. Thus, there has developed a whole literature on the social problems created by defects or handicaps and particularly on the families of handicapped children[4] and with the place of the handicapped in the community, especially the employment prospects for those who have passed through special education.[5] The employability of the handicapped has been an overriding concern since the time of the Egerton Commission, who wrote that: 'It is better for the state to expand its funds on the elementary technical education of the blind, than to have to support them through life in idleness' (Egerton Commission, 1889), through to the Warnock Committee who noted that: 'a small amount of extra help for school leavers . . . may enable them to hold down a job and reduce the chance of them entering a cycle of frequent changes of job, leading to long-term unemployment and dependence on social and psychiatric services' (*Special Educational Needs* . . ., 1978, p. 163).

Within the functional approach two uses of sociology may be discerned – these are the use of the social survey, concerned with documenting the extent and type of handicap or 'special need',

and the social problem approach, concerned with the organisation, management, provision for, and direction of, the handicapped or special child. It is not surprising that these two uses *became*
sociology for special education. Until the 1950s, sociology was
closely associated with the London School of Economics, where
understanding social life through surveys and statistics and a
Fabian-influenced concern with social problems and social
reform were dominant.

The early days of special educational provision were marked by
a need to know how many? what sort of problem? what to do
about it? and the survey/social problem approach provided some
answers. Thus, Tredgold in 1908 included a chapter on sociology
in his book, and considered that the Royal Commission of 1904–8
on the care and control of the feeble-minded had provided 'the
first important contribution to the sociology of mental deficiency'
since it documented possible numbers of defectives. Tredgold's
chapter included a discussion of numbers of 'aments', that is,
defective people, and the social problems they presented in terms
of employability, reliance on public assistance, crime, illegitimacy
and other 'vice' and the prevention of mental deficiency by segregation and sterilisation.

The survey tradition has persisted in special education, since
knowledge of the extent and distribution of handicapping conditions is regarded as essential in order to calculate resources and
make provision. Thus, Lewis made a further investigation for the
Wood Committee (Wood Report, 1929) to estimate numbers of
mental defectives, and the Isle of Wight survey (Rutter *et al.*,
1970) carried on the survey traditions to estimate that 16 per cent
of children in their middle school years had one or more handicaps. The Warnock Committee used evidence from the Isle of
Wight study, Rutter's ILEA research (Rutter *et al.*, 1975), the
National Child Development Study (Kellmer-Pringle *et al.*, 1966)
and their own specially commissioned study (Laing *et al.*, 1976) to
estimate that 'one in five children at some time during their
school career will require some form of special education' (*Special
Educational Needs* . . ., 1978, p. 41).

It is interesting to note that each survey during the twentieth
century has progressively discovered more and more children
with defects, handicaps or special needs, and it hardly needs to be
pointed out that numbers depend on the definition of the categ-

ory; as Rutter noted (Rutter *et al*., 1970): 'How many handicapped children one finds in a survey will depend largely on the criteria of handicap adopted.'

While it might appear that some handicaps are easier to define than others, this is not necessarily so. Ballantyne, in his book on deafness (1977), wrote: 'There *is* no satisfactory definition of degrees of deafness', and went on to point out that one of the best estimates of deafness in the general population comes from a government survey on hearing aids in 1947. If the definition of deafness is problematic, how much more so will definitions of, say, maladjustment, autism or educational subnormality be?

The functional assumptions behind these survey traditions are unproblematic – numbers must be known, so that provision can be made for the good of those with special needs. Comparative studies of special education are often presented from the survey provision perspective. For example, the Taylors' book on the handicapped in India (Taylor and Taylor, 1970) records the incidence of handicap (despite their note that 'there are as yet no official state or national arrangements for the collection of statistical data on the handicapped in India') and documents provision. Likewise, the functional assumptions behind the social problems approach preclude much questioning of definitions. MacMaster's brief chapter on the contribution of sociology, in one of the few books to attempt a theory of mental handicap (MacMaster, 1973), finds that sociology can analyse the family and the special schools. But in his view the family of the handicapped child needs analysis primarily to discover their reactions to having a handicapped child, and the school needs analysis primarily from the point of view of child management and school organisation.

A major problem with the functionalist approach in sociology is that it is based on consensus in society as being the normal state of affairs, conflict cannot really be explained other than in an evolutionary manner. In much of the literature on special education conflict is absent. It is assumed that all are working for 'the good of the child', and relationships between the various groups and professionals involved are considered to be a matter of smooth teamwork. The functionalist tradition views special education as a social problem, and not as a sociological problem, and there is a crucial difference between these two views. The way in which social situations attain the status of social problem is itself a subject for study within sociology (Spectre and Kitsuse, 1977). Social problems attract the attention of other people who wish to remedy them; they have a subjective, moral element in that the problems appear to threaten an established order or do not conform to the interests of particular groups in a society. A social problem orientation is not the best way to try to understand the development, organisation and change in special education. There are other ways, other sociological perspectives, which could perhaps be more illuminating.

New perspectives

Sociology, and particularly the sociology of education, has over the last ten years produced a variety of alternative perspectives, theories, approaches and methods which illuminate the educational arrangements made in our society. As Eggleston (1979) has pointed out:

> It is now possible to see the over-simplification of the earlier
> sociological view of the world as running smoothly, with
> agreed norms of behaviour, with institutions and individuals
> performing functions that maintained society and where even
> conflict was restricted to agreed areas.

It has become commonplace within sociology to note that sociologists have been freed from over-reliance on positivistic quantitative methodologies, and that functionalist views of society have been augmented by a variety of conflict and interpretative approaches, (Karabel and Halsey, 1977). The conflict approaches stem particularly from neo-Marxist writings, and the interpretative approaches have developed from, and alongside, phenomenological traditions. Thus the new perspectives which could be brought to bear are: first, those concerned with the nature of the historical development, and the economic, political and social climates in which special education developed, and how these developments contribute towards the reproduction of a given social order in society, and second, those relating to the social construction and maintenance of the world of special education and the interactions of the social participants.

From structural perspectives, questions could be raised about the whole development and purpose of special education in a class-stratified industrial society. Sociologists who used these perspectives would maintain that, since conflict is endemic in all social institutions, special education is no exception. There is conflict in a variety of situations in special education, not least within professions, between professionals, between parents and professionals in special schools, and between mainstream and special schooling; and power and coercion play a large part in resolving conflicts.

Conflict theories in education stem from the works of Marx and Weber, and while this is not the place to expand on their writings, it is important to stress the differences between their views, as they do provide the basis for the two major conflict approaches towards a study of social institutions and processes. While Marx was primarily interested in analysing social conflict in terms of class and labour-market, Weber showed that the domination of one group over another could occur in a variety of ways, and that a key concept in domination is authority. It is the acceptance of legitimate authority, as well as outright coercion, that ensures the compliance of some groups to others. This is an important notion in explaining why, for example, parents have come to accept professional judgment and opinion as to what 'is best' for their children. In a discussion of education (Weber, 1972) Weber showed how group interests penetrate the education system and how dominant interest groups can shape the structures of education for their own purpose. Thus, from this perspective sociologists could analyse the development of special education and its changes in terms of the conflicts between government and practitioners, or between professional groups.

Neo-Marxist conflict perspectives in education centre on the notion that a given educational structure is the outcome of political and ideological struggles between social classes, that class interests are behind any given pattern of educational organisation and that it is not possible to understand the working of any part of the education system independently of the class structure. Two important contributors to neo-Marxist sociological theory are Bowles and Gintis (1977) who have theorised about the role of education in the reproduction of the social division of labour, and – importantly for analysis of special education – have attacked the role of IQ measurement in assessment processes. They regard IQ more as a mechanism for the legitimation of inequality than as saying much about an individual's intellectual capacity.

Similarly, the work of Bourdieu and Passeron (1977) is concerned with the function of the education system in legitimating and perpetuating a given social order, by making social hierarchies appear to be based on gifts or merits. They argue that while educational advancement is based on ostensibly fair testing, the system demands a cultural competence not possessed by many families in society. From this perspective it no longer seems surprising that the mildly mentally handicapped or the educationally subnormal in society are predominantly lower-class. The large amount of literature which simply presents this as a 'fact' (Stein and Susser, 1960; Williams and Gruber, 1967; Gulliford, 1971) and the *assumption* that the lower social classes have a natural tendency to be more educationally retarded can be challenged from this perspective.

It is from these kinds of historical conflict perspectives that questions can be asked about the needs of a society that has developed and expanded a whole sub-system of education called 'special'. It becomes possible to turn rhetoric about the 'special needs' of children around, and ask what are the needs and interests of particular groups in the society that have influenced the development of special education, and what kinds of conflicts lie behind new developments?

This book is particularly concerned to ask some of the following questions, which will provide a context for the discussions held in each chapter:

(a) In whose interests did special education actually develop? Do the social origins lie more in the interests of ordinary education?

(b) Why did complicated categories of handicap and processes of selection and assessment develop? How were these processes legitimated? And why, having developed mechanisms to exclude children, is a debate on integration into normal education now taking place?

(c) How is the system of administration of special education linked to the use of professional expertise? And are the vested interests of expanding groups of professionals and practitioners served by the discovery of more and more children with 'special needs'?

(d) What are the goals of special education and why is curriculum theory and practice in this area so undeveloped?

(e) Are some types of special schooling more a form of control for particular groups of children? Why have black children been over-placed in ESN-M schooling, and can the treatment of ethnic minority children in special education illuminate its goals and purposes?

(f) What are the purposes of proposed expansion in special education?

The variety of interpretative and phenomenological approaches in sociology is also available to ask questions about special education. Phenomenologists stress the way in which social reality is a creation of social participants, and that social categories and social knowledge are not given or natural, but are socially constructed – a product of conscious communications and action between people. They tend to be preoccupied with the micro-world, examining how people make and remake the social world by their own interpretations and actions (Berger and Luckmann, 1971). The application of phenomenological perspectives to education opened up new empirical possibilities, as researchers were able to 'take as problematic', things that had previously been taken for granted. The major preoccupations of the 'new' sociologists of education have tended to be the class-room and teacher-pupil interaction (Woods, 1979), the curriculum, and knowledge. It is surprising that so far sociologists have shown little interest in applying these perspectives to special education. Deviancy theory and labelling theory (Becker, 1963; Downes, 1966) would also seem to be perspectives from which those categorised as 'in need' of special education can be regarded as deviating from behaviour required in ordinary education. Becker considered that 'the deviant is the one to whom that label has successfully been applied' (Becker, 1963). Special education provides more problematic 'labels' than any other part of the education system, many of which, for historical reasons, carry a stigma of inferiority and low status, and studies from deviancy perspectives might prevent simplistic acceptance of categories and labels.

There are some studies which have been carried out from interpretative perspectives, but usually from the point of view of the handicapped in society generally, rather than specifically applied to special education. Scott, using Goffman's notion of stigma, discussed the treatment of the handicapped by professionals (Scott, 1970). Dexter, as early as 1958, questioned the 'social problem' approach to mental deficiency (Dexter, 1958) and Spectre and Kitsuse, in studying how social situations attained the status of social problem, examined the use of the category 'moron' in the USA (Spectre and Kitsuse, 1977). Barton, in a paper to the twenty-first anniversary conference of the British Society for Mental Subnormality, applied Goffman's notion of 'total institution' to a study of the 'institutionalised mind' (Barton, 1973).

Given that we know very little about the workings and functions of all types of special schools, teachers, teacher-pupil interactions and negotiation, special school curriculum, the 'knowledge' that is deemed to be suitable for special schools, and the treatment and experiences of pupils and their parents – there are a variety of questions that could form the basis for research and study from interactionist perspectives. One question with which this book will concern itself particularly is: what are the experiences of pupils and teachers in special schools, given the negative emphasis of special schooling, which stress *in*capacity and *in*ability, and how are parents treated in special education?

The new perspectives and approaches suggested here provide what is loosely called macro and micro analysis in sociology. But while it is useful, particularly in research, to differentiate between levels of analysis – classroom or clinic, school, community, society – in practice these levels are not distinct. Some of the more recent work in the sociology of education has been devoted to demonstrating just how classroom activities are related to wider social processes (Woods, 1980 a and b).

The relevance of sociological perspectives

The established disciplines and practitioners in special education might very well ask what relevance sociological perspectives have, given that sociology can only provide perspectives, not tools for action. Debates on relevance have a long history and one connected to debates about the professional role of the sociologist in society (Shils, 1968; Rex, 1973).

Sociology in not institutionalised, that is, it is not a discipline recognised as useful by those who run society, and it is too prone to look critically at existing social orders and their supporting ideologies to be anything other than threatening to some. But if a claim is to be made that sociological perspectives are important in special education, then a case will have to be made for relevance. McNamara has recently argued a case for the removal of the sociology of education from initial teacher training, on the grounds that it is irrelevant (McNamara, 1977). He argues that teachers are concerned with particular and concrete social settings, that some sociological models are over-deterministic, and that sociological abstractions can confuse teachers and be counter-productive. While these arguments may well be valid, they do not provide a watertight case against the exclusion of sociological perspectives either from mainstream teacher training or from the training of all student professionals who may practise in special education. One of the reasons for the underdevelopment of curriculum in special schools is precisely because teachers have been more concerned with the practical immediate – 'what to do' – than with thinking about the wider goals of special education. Why do special school teachers do what they do in classrooms? On McNamara's second point, psychological and medical perspectives in special education can also easily become deterministic, especially as the stress is on individual causation. Sociology is not the only discipline which makes for determinism.

On the third point that McNamara makes, abstractions, concepts and 'jargon' in other disciplines may also confuse and irritate practitioners, and be counter-productive. There is no reason for sociology to be singled out for exclusion.

However, since sociology *has* by and large been excluded from the initial education of all professionals and practitioners in special education, justification here must be made for inclusion, not exclusion, from training courses. Relevance, of course, means different things to different people, and while student practitioners might be more interested in the short-term relevance of sociological perspectives, other people might be more interested in long-term relevance.

Kellman has pointed out that what is considered relevant 'is a matter of judgment depending, as in other things, on the time perspective used' (Kellman, 1970).

In the short term sociology obviously cannot offer any immediate tools for the clinic or classroom, in terms of, say, test procedures or curriculum materials, but even in the short term sociological perspectives should help all students planning to practise in special education.

First, it should help students to question critically the concepts presented to them by other disciplines, and from other viewpoints. For example, much of the descriptive literature on the development of special education asks students to accept that both statutory and non-statutory categories of handicap have gradually evolved, as though spontaneously, over the last hundred years, and that the major problem is matching the categorisations of handicaps, or 'needs', to children. Sociological analysis has begun to show that administrative categories, particularly those that remove children from mainstream education, do not mysteriously develop in an evolutionary manner. Categories appear, change and disappear because of the goals pursued and the decisions made, by people who control the special educational processes. As a second example, psychological approaches may teach that behaviour modification is a tool for dealing with educationally subnormal children. Sociological perspectives can help students to ask wider social and political questions about the power of some groups to 'modify' the behaviour of other, weaker groups in a society.

A second way in which sociological perspectives can have immediate relevance is by making explicit the possible development of psychological or sociological myths of 'intractable causation' (Hargreaves, 1972; Meighan, 1981) by which a child's deficiency or handicap comes to be explained in deterministic terms. Practitioners may regard labels such as 'low IQ', 'organic handicap', 'deprived background' as adequate causal explanations for a child's being in special education. Literature which subsumes mildly educationally subnormal children under the label 'disadvantaged child' is helping to create this kind of myth for all the children. If fatalistic psychological views of individual causality or simple sociological views of environmental determinism go unchallenged, the practice of teaching in special schools will be extremely limited. McNamara blames the teaching of sociology for these kinds of simplistic sociological assumptions. But, in fact, it is other disciplines that often perpetuate environmental determinism. Psychological acceptance of poor environment determining the mild retardation of lower-class children can be traced in (psychological) writings from Burt (1937) to Gulliford (1969).

A third way in which sociology can be immediately relevant, particularly to students planning to teach in special education, is to show that teachers are applied sociologists. They use group situations to attempt to change the behaviour of children and they work within social settings and intricate social relationships. It is their definition and beliefs about the types of children they teach, and the actions they perform on the basis of these beliefs, that make the reality of a 'class of maladjusted pupils' or the 'achievement' of a severely subnormal child. Sociology can show that people do define social situations, and it is their actions which help to perpetuate and determine social arrangements.

The longer-term relevance of sociological perspectives applies to all those involved in special education, particularly the clients – parents and children. One of the uses of sociology, as previously noted, is to demystify, to provide ordinary people with tools to ask what is going on, and some knowledge of the way people with power keep and legitimate their power. Special education has developed as one of the most secret areas of education, partly because of the medical connections, and the ideology of 'medical confidentiality'.

At times the procedures are so secret that even other professionals are not informed (Tomlinson, 1981), but the secrecy also has to do with the way in which the professional people regard parents. The reluctance of some parents to co-operate in the admission of their children to special schools earlier in the century, meant the creation of a 'certification' process, and no changes in 'enforceable procedures' are envisaged in the future. Parents can be coerced into sending their children into special education and need be told little about the procedures. The Warnock Report, reviewing record-keeping, has suggested two types of personal folder for each child. The second folder 'is needed for the results of professional consultation and sensitive information . . . about a child's social background or family relationships. This should be a confidential folder . . . kept in school, and access to it controlled by the head-teacher' (*Special Educational Needs* . . ., 1978, p. 56).

Parents, it seems, can be denied access to information pertaining to themselves and their 'special' children and to be denied knowledge is to be denied power. There is already evidence (Booth, 1978; Tomlinson, 1981) to indicate that many parents in special education feel inadequately consulted and involved and feel mystified by professionals. They do not know the limits of secrecy or accountability on the part of the professionals. They *are* a weaker social group, in terms of control over their own and their children's destiny. Sociological perspectives can analyse structures of power and the way power is legitimated through secrecy, non-accountability, persuasion and coercion. Sociology 'may not be able to influence the powerful – but it may be able to help the alienated and the puzzled' (Rex, 1974, p. 233).

It was C. Wright Mills who first made a distinction between public issues and private troubles. He wrote that 'men do not usually define the troubles they endure in terms of historical change and institutional contradiction' (Wright Mills, 1959, pp. 14–15). Troubles are usually defined by individuals as their own problem and often their own 'fault'. Issues are social property – they transcend the environment of the individual. But there *is* a relationship between personal troubles and public issues, although those with power try to confuse the two. Those in charge of special education do have vested interests in defining problems as purely private troubles for individual families. This is one reason why psychology is so influential in special education – it tends to consider individuals as divorced from wider social contexts. But special education *is* a public issue, a social process which is available for analysis and for 'de-mystification'.

Another important aspect of the analysis of structures and processes in special education would be to examine the difference between rhetoric and practice. There is a good deal of rhetoric and exhortation in special education, but there is often a difference between statement of interest and practice. Sociology can attempt to analyse the difference between complacement rhetoric and actual practice.

A further long-term relevance of sociology could be in the area of the discussion of development and change. More than any other part of the education system, special education appears to be in a permanently dynamic state, continually changing, expanding or abolishing categories of handicap, arguing about provision and the allocation of resources, expanding numbers and types of professional and other personnel. Sociological perspectives can indicate that education systems and their parts do, in fact, change because of power struggles and vested interests. New legislation, as envisaged in the government white paper (Department of Education and Science, 1980b) on *Special Needs in Education*, will result in some further changes of form, provision of resources, and organisation in special education. Since these changes will affect the lives of thousands of children, sociology should develop analyses which will have relevance to social events of this importance.

The sociological perspective referred to in this chapter, then, corresponds to what Wright Mills called the sociological imagination. If those involved in special education come to think in wider historical, social and political terms about what they are doing, rather than going about their work with a rigid set of procedures loosely labelled 'educational', they will understand more clearly what they are doing, and be able to improve practice. The parents of children in special education, relatively powerless in the processes, could, using sociological perspectives, be better equipped to make their own assessment of the situation, orient themselves in the processes and gain more control over their own and their children's lifestyles. The promise of the sociological imagination is to help people understand the interrelationship between history and individual lives, between the so-called private and the public. This imagination is urgently needed in special education to examine the way in which the private trouble of having produced, or being, a child with special needs, and the resultant referral, assessment, labelling and diagnosing, *is* related to the wider social structure, to processes of social and cultural reproduction, and to the ideologies and rationalisations which are produced to mystify the participants, and often, to perplex the practitioners.

Chapter Two · The social origins of special education

A study of the history of special education in England has not attracted many scholars, and the social origins of special education remain obscure. Part of this neglect may be explained by the difficulty in probing beyond the powerful ideology of benevolent humanitarianism as being a major force which motivated and continues to motivate government, professionals and practitioners to identify more and more children as in need of special education.

The aim of this chapter is to examine the development of special education in the light of prevailing social, economic and professional interests rather than in terms of an ideology of humanitarian progress.

State provision for universal ordinary elementary education was established some 110 years ago by the acts of 1870, 1876 and 1880. State provision for special education in England and Wales is usually dated from 1874, when the London School Board established a separate class for the deaf, or from 1893, when the Elementary Education (Blind and Deaf Children) Act laid the duty on local authorities to provide separate education for these children. By the early 1890s the word 'special' was in general usage, as the first classes and schools for Special Instruction for Defective Children had been set up in Leicester and London.

The literature documenting the emergence of provision has tended to concentrate on the descriptive detail of acts, commissions and provision involved, within the assumption that more provision equals progress. Pritchard's much-quoted study provides an example of this. After a careful factual examination of the development of special education from 1760 he wrote, 'progress there has been . . . progress there must yet be' (Pritchard, 1963). The Warnock Committee relied heavily on Pritchard's work to produce their chapter on the historical background of special education and wrote:

> as with ordinary education, education for the handicapped began with individual and charitable enterprise. There followed in time the intervention of government, first to support voluntary effort and make good deficiencies through state provision, and finally, to create a national framework in which public and voluntary agencies could act in partnership to see that all children, whatever their disability, received a suitable education. The framework reached its present form only in this decade. (*Special Education Needs* . . ., 1978 p. 8.)

This kind of statement, stressing the 'charitable' and the intervention of government to 'make good' deficiencies, creates the impression of spontaneous development from purely humanitarian motives. It precludes discussing other possible motives of those responsible for the development of special education, and considering conflict and power struggles during development.

It is worth stressing here, again, that education systems and their parts do not develop spontaneously, or in an evolutionary manner, and they do not develop out of purely humanitarian motives. They develop because it is in the interests of particular groups in a society that they should develop, and that they should develop in particular ways. Further, as Archer has pointed out, what actually becomes 'education' is seldom the realisation of some ideal form of instruction. There never was any 'ideal' form of special education envisaged, towards which a benevolent government has been working, instead 'most of the forms that education takes are the political products of power struggles' (Archer, 1979, p. 3). The forms that special education have taken in the past and take today are the products of particular vested interests in the society, and one of the most noticeable characteristics of the history of special education has been power struggles between medical, psychological and educational personnel, who all have an interest in dominating definitions of special education. Existing historical accounts of special education tend to leave out notions of conflict, vested interests and consideration of the wider social motives and expediency which dictated that a special education system should emerge. A sociological discussion must surely look at historical 'facts' with these notions in mind. There is the danger, however, that, lacking proper historical training, sociologists will simply select facts to fit their ideas. Analytical modes of appraising the facts are certainly lacking in the history of special education. However, sociologists can point out that there have been, throughout the twentieth century, growing doubts about the inevitability and definition of progress and that the acceptance of evolutionary arguments has become less academically respectable.

The treatment of those who are socially defined as defective or handicapped is certainly dependent on the values and interests of dominant groups[1] in particular societies. For example, the ancient Greeks and the Nazi party in Germany in the 1930s shared similar values concerning racial purity, and killed handicapped children who were thought to interfere with this purity. In Protestant England the value placed on productive work has tended to dominate the treatment of the handicapped. The 1601 Elizabethan Poor Law provided 'the necessary relief of the lame, impotent, old, blind, and such others' only if they could not work, and disabled children were, if possible, put out to be apprentices. Millowners in the 1800s took quotas of idiot children among pauper children supplied for their mills by the workhouses (Pritchard, 1963), and the brief of the Warnock Report was not only to review educational provision for the handicapped, but also 'to consider arrangements to prepare them for employment' (*Special Educational Needs* . . ., 1978).

What is taken as 'individual and charitable enterprise' is also related to values and interests in society; it is seldom the product of pure altruism and disinterested humanitarianism. The early pioneers of special education are often presented in highly individualistic charismatic terms, as though they were acting out of a social context and counter to existing trends. Itard, probably one of the best known personalities in the history of special education, is presented as having made the first 'scientific' attempt to educate the subnormal, by training Victor, the Wild Boy of Aveyron (Itard, 1894). But Itard was himself a representative of eighteenth-century interest in science and medicine, and his pioneering work with Victor contributed to medical claims to dominance in the education of the subnormal.

Individuals are influenced and constrained by prevailing cultural values and social interests, they do not singlehandedly alter events through altruism. This is not to deny that motives of compassion and humanitarianism play a part, but accounts of the social origins of special education must go further to seek another interests. For example, Thomas Braidwood, celebrated as a pioneer in the education of the deaf, was inspired by commercial interests to keep his oral method of instruction a secret. An American teacher, arriving in 1815 to learn the method, found all teachers of the deaf pledged to secrecy (Hodgson, 1953). One reason for the charisma surrounding personalities concerned with special education is that their 'clients' have seldom been in a situation to present an alternative viewpoint regarding the humanitarianism of their mentors. Mary Dendy, pioneering the life-long segregation of the feeble-minded in Cheshire in the early 1900s, was perhaps more concerned with 'stemming the great evil of feeble-mindedness in our country' than with the happiness of her charges (*Report of the Royal Commission on the Care and Control of the Feeble-Minded*, 1908, evidence of Miss Dendy, vol. 1, p. 39).

Thus, although pre-state special educational provision might appear to be divorced from social interests, and solely the product of individual and charitable acts, this is by no means the case. Wider social and economic interests were involved. Interests which particularly affected the provision of early forms of special education were the economic and commercial interests of a developing industrial society, which required as many people as possible to be productive, and political ruling-class interests in maintaining order and control in society – since defective people have usually been identified with potentially troublesome groups in society. The vested interests of professional groups, particularly medical men, were important in the provision of pre-state special education, although it was with the development of state special education that other professional vested interests became more important.

Sociologically, the history of special education must be viewed in terms of the benefits it brought for a developing industrial society, the benefits for the normal mass education system of a 'special' sub-system of education, and the benefits that medical, psychological, educational and other personnel derived from encouraging new areas of professional expertise. It will be useful at this point to chart a chronology of selected events concerned with the development of special education to provide a framework for a sociological discussion of this development.

Selected events in special education

1760   Thomas Braidwood opens the Academy for the Deaf and Dumb in Edinburgh.

1791   Rev. Henry Dannett opens the School of Instruction for the Indigent Blind, Liverpool.

1792   Thomas Watson (Braidwood's nephew) opens London Asylum for the Blind at Bermondsey, then on the Old Kent Road.

1793   Asylum for the Blind opens in Edinburgh and Bristol, with trade training.

1799   London School for the Indigent Blind opened by four businessmen to instruct the blind in a trade.

1799   Itard, in France, begins work with Victor, the 'Wild Boy of Aveyron'.

1805   Asylum for the Blind opens in Norwich.

1809   Braidwood Asylum for the Deaf opens at Margate, Kent. Watson publishes his *Instruction of the Deaf and Dumb.*

1825   School for the Deaf opens in Manchester, financed by a banker, Robert Phillips.

1825   School for the Deaf opens in Liverpool, financed by a businessman, Edward Conner.

1826   West of England Institution for the Deaf and Dumb opens in Exeter.

1826   School for the Deaf opened in Doncaster.

1833   School for the Blind opened in York.

1833   First State intervention in education – £20,000 given to the National Society and the British and Foreign Schools Society. None spent on the handicapped.

1838   London School for Teaching the Blind to Read opened (for middle- and upper-class children).

1838   School for Blind and Deaf opened in Newcastle. Separate provision made after ten years of disputes.

1839   Manchester School for the Blind opened, funded by an Oldham merchant, Thomas Henshaw.

1841 Catholic Blind Asylum opened in Liverpool by Sisters of Charity of St Vincent de Paul.

1841 Institute for Blind and Deaf opened in Bath – closed 1896.

1842 Asylums for the Deaf and Blind opened in Brighton.

1846 The Misses White Open School for Idiots in Bath.

1847 Park House Asylum for Idiots opened at Highgate by Dr Andrew Reed, non-conformist minister. 1858 moved to Redhill.

1847 Royal Cambrian Institute for the Deaf and Dumb opens in Aberystwyth.

1847 School for the Deaf opens in Bristol.

1847 General Institute for the Blind opens in Birmingham, funded by William Harold, a merchant.

1851 Cripples' Home and Industrial School for Girls opens at Marylebone, London.

1859 Eastern Counties Asylum for Idiots opened at Colchester.

1864 Jewish School for the Deaf opened in Whitechapel.

1864 Western Counties Asylum for Idiots opened at Starcross, Devon.

1864 Northern Counties Asylum for Idiots (The Royal Albert) opened at Lancaster.

1865 National Industrial Home for Crippled Boys opened in Kensington, London.

1867 Metropolitan Poor Act, First state-run Idiot and Imbecile Asylums set up in Surrey and Hertfordshire.

1868 Thomas Armitage founded the British and Foreign Association for promoting the Education and Employment of the Blind (later the RNIB).

1869 Charity Organisation Society set up.

1870 Education Act established the principle of mass elementary education.

1870 Midland Counties Asylum opened at Knowle, near Birmingham.

1874 First School Board Class for Deaf opened in Bethnal Green.

1874 Hampstead Asylum for Idiots – state-run, set up. 1875 moved to Darenth.

1885 Royal Commission on the Blind, Deaf and Dumb set up (the Egerton Commission).

1886   Idiots Act separated idiots and imbeciles from lunatics.

1888   Dr Shuttleworth, Superintendent of the Lancaster Asylum, publishes a paper on 'The Education of Children of Abnormally Weak Mental Capacity', *Journal of Mental Science*, vol. 34. Appeal for 'Auxiliary Classes and Schools' for children 'not irretrievably deficient'.

1888   Invalid Children's Aid Association set up.

1889   Report of the Royal Commission on Blind, Deaf, Dumb and others.

1890   London School Board prepares a scheme for special schools and classes.

1892   First Special Class opened in Leicester. Followed by three Schools for Special Instruction in London.

1893   Charity Organisation Society publish *The Feeble-minded Child and Adult* – a demand for state special schools.

1896   Poor Law School Committee Report draws on Dr Warner's Survey of 100,000 children to declare 'from various causes we are ever increasing the accumulation of defective and afflicted children in our schools' – and calls for special schools.

1896   National Association for Promoting the Welfare of the Feeble-Minded set up – Dr Tredgold a member.

1896   Committee on Defective and Epileptic Children set up by Education Department Chairman, Rev. Sharpe, HMI.

1898   Report of Committee on Defective and Epileptic Children – assessment of children for special school to be a 'team' decision (medical officer, class teacher, head of special school). Schools to give six hours a week manual training and prepare feeble-minded children for employment.

1899   Elementary Education (Defective and Epileptic Children) Act. Local authorities urged – not required – to make provision for special instruction.

1903   Association of Teachers in Special Schools set up.

1904   Establishment of delicate schools for semi-invalid children.

1904   Royal Commission on the Care and Control of the Feeble-Minded set up. Report recommended that all feeble-minded children should come under a Board of Control, rather than the Board of Education.

1907   School Medical Service set up.

1907   College of Teachers of Blind set up.

1907   In Bristol opening of a class for the partially deaf. In London opening of a class for the partially sighted.

1908   Tredgold published first edition of *Mental Deficiency*.

1913   12,000 'defective' children in 177 special schools, plus voluntary provision. 175 education authorities had made some state provision.

1913   Mental Deficiency Act. Education authorities given the duty of ascertaining which children aged 7–16 were defective.

1913   Cyril Burt appointed by London County Council as first psychologist.

1914   Elementary Education (Defective and Epileptic Children) Act. Local authorities required to make provision for mentally defective children.

1918   Clause in Fisher Education Act lays duty on local authorities to provide education for the physically defective.

1920   All special schools to be inspected by the Medical Branch of the Board of Education.

1921   National Institute for Blind opened a Sunshine Home at Chorleywood and established Chorleywood Grammar School for Girls.

1921   Education Act – enabled local authorities to compel parents of 'certified' children to send them to special schools.

1924   Joint Departmental Committee on Mental Deficiency set up (Wood Committee).

1926   First Child Guidance Clinic set up.

1927   Board of Education circular 1388 advised that 'it did not seem prudent to incur heavy expenditure at the present moment on new schools for feeble-minded children'.

1929   Wood Committee recommended that a larger group of 'retarded' children join the educable defective and be educated, without certification, in a 'helpful variant of the ordinary school'.

1939   17,000 children in state special schools.

1944   Education Act. Local education authorities had a duty to ascertain children suffering from 'a disability of body or mind' and to provide 'special educational treatment' in special schools or elsewhere.

1945 Handicapped pupils and health service regulations defined eleven categories of handicap (modified to ten in 1953). HP forms introduced.

1946 Ministry of Education pamphlet no. 5, *Special Educational Treatment,* defines the categories of handicap.

1955 Underwood Committee on maladjusted children reported.

1956 Ministry of Education pamphlet no. 30, *Education of Handicapped Pupils*, reviewed provision over ten years.

1965 Department of Education and Science publishes a report on *Special Education Today*, Report on Education no. 23.

1968 Summerfield Report *Psychologists in the Education Services*.

1970 The Education (Handicapped Children) Act brought severely subnormal children into education.

1970–1 Race Relations Board investigate Haringey LEA as to the numbers of West Indian children ascertained as ESN-M. Bernard Coard publishes 'How the West Indian Child is made ESN in the British School System'.

1972 Vernon Report. Report of the Committee of Enquiry into the Education of the Visually Handicapped.

1973 DES Report on Education no. 77, *Special Education – A Fresh Look.*

1973 Letter to Chief Education Officers from the DES on the educational arrangements for immigrant children who may need special education.

1973 Warnock Committee set up to inquire into the education of handicapped children and young people.

1974 Association of Special Education, College of Special Education, Guild of Backward Teachers merge to form the National Council for Special Education. Journal, *Special Education – Forward Trends.*

1975 DES issues circular 2/75. This looked at 'The Discovery of Children Requiring Special Education and the Assessment of their Needs'. HP forms were to be superseded by SE forms.

1976 Education Act, included Section 10. Suggested laying a duty on LEAs to provide special education in normal schools when it is practicable. This section was never implemented.

1978 HMI Survey of behavioural units found that 239 special units for disruptive children had been set up in 69 of the 96 LEAs in England.

1978 Warnock Committee reports recommended that statutory categories of handicap be abolished in favour of assessment of 'special educational needs' although descriptive labels may be retained. The ESN category to be merged with remedial children to become children with learning difficulties.

1979 180,000 children in state special schools. 15,774 in non-state special education.

1980 White Paper, *Special Needs in Education*, recommends the abolition of categories of handicap and the introduction of a 'broad definition of special educational needs'. Introduces the notion of 'recorded' and 'non-recorded' children. No money available to implement any recommendations; legislation proposed for 1981.

1981 International year of the disabled. 1981 Education Act. A child has 'special educational needs' if he has a learning difficulty which calls for special educational provision. LEAs must 'make and maintain' a statement to record children with special needs.

Special education before 1900

By the early nineteenth century education for the mass of the people was becoming regarded as a necessary discipline for controlling potential unrest amongst the working classes and also to produce a literate population to further commercial interests. England did have an education system – privately owned and dominated by the Anglican church – but Archer (1979) has pointed out that the developing capitalist economy was being hindered by Anglican definitions of instruction, which placed little stress on commercial values, although, on the other hand, ruling groups needed religious influence as a form of social quietism for working-class unrest. However, neither the Anglican-dominated National Society for Educating the Poor in the Principles of the Established Church, nor the non-conformist British and Foreign Schools Society – the pioneers of normal mass education – took any interest in the education of the defective or handicapped. Possibly, as Prichard has suggested (1963, p. 25), there were too few handicapped to warrent the expense of concentrating them in any form of sectarian special education, but certainly one of the interesting aspects of the development of special education is the lack of interest displayed by all religious denominations. It was businessmen who took an interest, since it was economic good sense to make as many citizens, even the handicapped, productive as possible. The profit-motive was an important interest in early special educational provision for the handicapped. For example, the Braidwood family, capitalising on Thomas Braidwood's talent for teaching the deaf, ran their Asylums for the Deaf as a business venture, first in Edinburgh, then in London, opening a branch school in Margate in 1809. As befitted capitalist enterprise of the time, profits were made by under-paying teachers and falsifying records (Hodgson, 1953). But, in the early schools for the deaf and the blind, commercial interests dominated and pupils were taught trades if possible. Businessmen were responsible for the creation of a number of deaf schools during the nineteenth century, occasionally motivated also by the misfortune of friends or relatives. Robert Phillips, a Manchester banker, taking an interest in the deaf daughter of a neighbour, raised money for a deaf school from business friends in Manchester in 1825, and a merchant, Edward Conner, shortly followed suit in Liverpool. The Rothschild family were influential in opening a Jewish deaf school in London in 1864. While the school did take poor children free of charge, Baroness Rothschild's royal connections initially encouraged money from the wealthy upper classes (Pritchard, 1963).

Although the first School of Instruction for the Indigent Blind was opened in Liverpool in 1791 by a clergyman, Henry Dannett, the object of the school was commercial. It was to 'render the blind useful to their country' by removing 'habits of idleness', and by 1800 the school had been re-named the School of Industry for the Blind. Those 'incapable of any labour' were discharged from the school. As with the deaf schools, several early nineteenth-

century blind schools were funded by businessmen and vocational and trade training was stressed. By 1793 there was a blind
school at Edinburgh, with workshops and the name of Asylum for
the Industrious Blind, and one at Bristol, also with trade and
vocational training. The London School for the Indigent Blind,
opening in 1799, had the sole object of instructing the blind in a
trade. Blindness and deafness were handicaps that were admitted to affect all social classes, unlike mental and to some extent
physical defects, which the middle and upper classes have often
been at some pains to conceal. By 1866 Worcester College had
been opened to ensure that 'blind children of opulent parents
might obtain an education suitable to their station in life'
(Thomas, 1957).

Religious organisations initially demonstrated little interest in
the handicapped, even the blind and deaf. Protestantism did not
originally have a history of kindness towards the handicapped;
Martin Luther considered that the subnormal were 'Godless',
and, as Pritchard (1963) noted, physical and mental handicap
were 'frequently taken to be an indication of divine displeasure'.
Catholicism had been kinder, particularly in France, where St
Vincent de Paul and his Sisters of Charity had included the
handicapped at their hospital at Bicêtre, but it was not until 1841
that the first Catholic school for the handicapped opened in
England – the Liverpool Catholic Blind Asylum. The two
societies, the National and the British and Foreign, did not concern themselves with the handicapped, and certainly none of the
first state grants of £20,000, given to the two societies by the
House of Commons in 1833, was spent on the handicapped. It is
likely that religious sectarian interests in bringing as many children as possible into Anglican, non-conformist or Catholic education in the nineteenth century meant that those handicapped
children who were not too defective were simply accepted to
enlarge the sectarian school population. Certainly, after the
introduction of compulsory state education, voluntary religious
schools had vested interests in continuing to encourage all children to attend their ordinary elementary schools if possible.

After the beginning of state education, economic interests in
making as many of the blind and deaf self-sufficient and employable became more pronounced. There was also a more overt
political interest in the social control of groups who might prove

troublesome to the hierarchical order of the society, because of their 'vice, folly or improvidence' (Egerton Commission, 1889). Accordingly, a Royal Commission on the Blind, Deaf, Dumb and Others was set up in 1885.

The chairman was an aristocrat, Lord Egerton, whose family had commercial interests in the West Indian sugar trade, and the brief of the Commission was frankly economic.

> The blind, deaf, dumb and the educable class of imbecile . . . if left uneducated become not only a burden to themselves but a weighty burden to the state. It is in the interests of the state to educate them, so as to dry up, as far as possible, the minor streams which must ultimately swell to a great torrent of pauperism. (Egerton Commission, 1889)

The Commission was illustrative of a crucial delemma concerning special education in a society dominated by a Protestant work ethic – how to make as many of the handicapped productive, while keeping the cost of any provision low so that central and local government do not have to use too much money provided by non-handicapped tax- and rate-payers. In 1889 the Commission reported that there should be separate school classes provided by the state for the blind and deaf and that after school they should receive technical or trade training. In 1893 the Elementary Education (Blind and Deaf Children) Act laid the duty on local school boards to provide appropriate education for blind and deaf children in their area.

Provision for the physically handicapped in the nineteenth century was also based on economic considerations. A Cripples' Home and Industrial School for girls was opened in London in 1851, and a National Industrial Home for Crippled Boys in 1865. The emphasis again was on vocational training although some school instruction was given. Expenses, as in any thrifty capitalist venture, were kept low by using voluntary non-paid teachers and non-handicapped girls from the Industrial School to do the domestic work (Bartley, 1871).

Provision in England for children who came to be known as mentally defective, subnormal, or retarded came towards the middle of the nineteenth century, although educationally it was not until 1944 that separate school provision was envisaged for mentally and physically defective children. Nineteenth-century care and provision for lower-class mentally handicapped and defective adults and children was much more the concern of those interested in order and control. But economic interests also featured in the care of the mentally handicapped. The tendency beginning in the seventeenth century, to confine paupers and the unemployed to the workhouse, had drawn in numbers of defective children who interrupted the smooth functioning of forced labour and set problems for the workhouse guardians. The move for asylum provision for defective poor children was largely to remove their troublesome presence from the workhouses. Until 1886 there was no legal distinction between the severely mentally defective idiots, and lunatics, both troublesome groups who had been confined to asylums from the early 1700s to maintain public order. By the mid 1800s the Lunacy Commission was arguing for a separation of the two groups, particularly as a higher grade of idiot, the imbecile, was by now considered to be capable of benefiting from some instruction. Thus, the setting up of separate institutions for the mentally defective, to give some kind of instruction and trade training, served a variety of interests. Economic interests were served by removing defective people who were interrupting the workhouse labour, but also the possibility of training mentally defective people for productive work was important. Political interests were served by the removal into residential care and confinement of a potentially disruptive social group.

But above all the medical profession, struggling for professional recognition in nineteenth-century Britain, developed an interest in mental defect, and the profession of medicine was considerably enhanced by medical claims to care for and control the mentally defective. This medical interest is often presented as divorced from other social interests of the time, but medical interest in the defective was by no means as self-evident as it appears now. A history of the British Medical Association noted that in 1840 'the future of medicine and surgery in Great Britain was to be decided by bargaining between the state and the profession' (Clark, 1964, ch. 24). The medical professions, throughout the 1840s and 1850s, had been urging the government to grant professional status and a closed professional organisation, and in 1858 the Medical Act established a National Register of practitioners. In return, as part of the bargain, it undoubtedly served state social and economic interests that the confinement, directed employment and, subsequently, education of mental defectives should be overseen by medical men. State and medical interests in mid-nineteenth-century England certainly coincided over the treatment of mentally defective people. Medical domination of the field has been so successful that up to the present time (1981) medical officers are the only people who have statutory powers to certify that a child has a 'disability' of the mind.

Medical opinion regarding mental defect was quite diverse during the nineteenth century, but two influences on medicine itself were the Darwinian evolutionary notions of physical development – Downs in 1866 explained 'Mongolism' as a state equivalent to the physiological development of the Mongolian race – and the passion for classification originally developed in biology. The expanding and re-workings of various classifications of defect and handicap over the past hundred years is partially due to medical influence.

One medical influence that had an important effect on general public beliefs about mental defect was the developing nineteenth-century interest in the possible hereditary nature of defect, which culminated in the eugenics movement, concerned with possible racial degeneration through the birth of defective children. Moves to segregate mentally defective adults and children on account of their possible danger to society very largely contributed to the stigma still attached to special schooling. The argument that defects were hereditary was strongly supported in the latter part of the nineteenth century by the work of Francis Galton (1869). He concluded that while exceptional intellect was hereditary, so too were feeble minds and criminal tendencies. Dugdale's (1910) study of the Juke family, purporting to show the disastrous social effects of the reproduction of five 'problem' sisters, and later Goddard's study of the Kallikak family (1912), strengthened beliefs in the links between mental defect, crime, unemployment, prostitution and other evils. Nineteenth-century industrialists and the political ruling class certainly had interests in suppressing all these vices.

The aim of the eugenicists was to improve the quality of the 'British race' by disallowing reproduction of defectives, by segregation or sterilisation. Tredgold, an enthusiastic supporter of eugenics, wrote in his influential book on *Mental Deficiency*, first published in 1908, that 'the bulk of primary defectives come from psychopathic stock' (Tredgold and Soddy, 1956, p. 399). The influence of the eugenics movement on the treatment of all defective or handicapped people, but particularly the mentally defective, reached its height in the early part of the twentieth century and certainly influenced the type and provision of education for all handicapped children.

The first Idiots' Asylums in England were voluntary, financed by fees and voluntary subscriptions, and by and large served the middle and upper classes. Andrew Reed, a non-conformist minister, motivated by a desire both to 'save the souls' of idiots and prevent them from becoming a 'burden to the state', opened an asylum at Highgate in 1848 – this moved to Redhill in 1855. Asylums opened at Colchester – the Eastern Counties Asylum in 1859, at Starcross in Devon – the Western Counties Asylum, and at Lancaster – the Northern Counties, in 1864, and at Knowle – the Midland counties, in 1870. The Lancaster Asylum, renamed the Royal Lancaster as the Queen was patron, charged between 50 and 200 guineas per annum, although also admitting some free cases.

Pauper idiots were largely confined to workhouses, although the need to remove them guaranteed state intervention, and in 1867 the Metropolitan Poor Act empowered the Metropolitan Asylums Board to make provisions for them. State asylums opened in Surrey and Hertfordshire and in 1874 at Hampstead. This last asylum moved in 1875 to Darenth, and illustrated the principle of cheap provision and the work ethic for the working-class 'defectives'. By 1887 only half the children were receiving any form of instruction and costs were low. Workshop blocks were used so that as many inmates as possible were productive. It was the medical superintendent of this asylum who reported to the Royal Commission of 1889 that every child was reaching its highest educational potential (Pritchard, 1963, ch. 2).

By the final quarter of the nineteenth century, commercial interests in the education of the working class had encouraged state intervention, and the needs of industrial capitalism were being better served by a workforce which was at least minimally educated. Political interests in the control of the potentially rebellious lower classes were also served by an elementary 'education for docility', although the middle and upper classes reserved the privileges of secondary and higher education for themselves. However, both commercial and political groups had interests in the selection of all 'defectives' out of state schooling, particularly of a large group of children who have always formed the largest group of those designated as 'handicapped'. These were the feeble-minded. These children became the educable defectives, then the educationally subnormal and finally 'children with learning difficulties', as the educational system struggled with larger numbers of children who could not, or would not, conform to the practices and goals of normal education.

It was the introduction of state compulsory education in the 1870s that focused attention more acutely on children who were not idiots or imbeciles, but who experienced difficulty within a formal education system. Again, state intervention in discovering these dull and troublesome children was not necessarily for their own 'good' or a recognition of their 'needs'. It was primarily to ensure the smoother running of the normal education system. The religious voluntary schools, anxious to retain as many of their pupils as possible as state education developed, may have had an interest in keeping handicapped children in their schools. State schools, working towards the standards required by the Payment by Results Scheme, had an interest in getting rid of these children. The children were not necessarily provided for because of state humanitarianism, but because their presence was troublesome.

The influences on the creation of special schools and classes for the feeble-minded appear diverse, but they are in fact limited and representative of the interests of certain groups. The Charity Organisation Society, a body founded in 1869 to co-ordinate charity and encourage 'thrift and self-help' in a society tending towards liberal reform and even state socialism, campaigned for special schools for the feeble-minded. The Egerton Commission on the Blind, Deaf and Dumb had considered the feeble-minded and had recommended special schooling. Medical men, in particular Warner, a London paediatrician, and Shuttleworth, Medical Superintendent of the Royal Albert Asylum, were campaigning for special schools overseen by doctors as 'the conditions of feeble-mindedness are so mixed up with physical conditions that it is important that a person who has been trained to discriminate between various abnormal physical conditions should have the decision' (quoted in Pritchard, 1963, p. 138). Educationalists, particularly the London School Board with the largest number of troublesome children, were also developing interests in ridding normal schools of the children and setting up special schools. Some of the linkages between these interests can be traced by noting individual contacts. The upper-class patrons of the COS included Lord Lichfield, the Earl of Derby, and seventeen peers who were vice-presidents in 1880. Lord Egerton, head of the 1889 Royal Commission, was a neighbour of Lord Lichfield. A number of individuals in the COS and on commissions and committees on defectives, had interests in the control of defective groups, particularly when the influence of eugenics began to link the defective to crime and unemployment. Sir Charles Trevelyan, secretary to the 1875 COS Committee on Idiots and Imbeciles, had, in the 1840s, helped to administer famine relief in Ireland, and considered death by starvation 'as discipline'. His recommendations on the separation of defective from normal children were in the interests of social control.

Meanwhile, medical and educational interests began to conflict openly with the setting up of special schools for the feeble-minded. Medical men had an advantage, in that they had come to dominate the asylum education of idiots and imbeciles. By the 1890s, the London School Board had 'prepared a scheme for special instruction in schools or classes, for children who by reason of mental or physical defects, cannot be properly taught in ordinary standards by ordinary methods', and the first schools for special instruction opened in London's poorest districts. Leicester opened a special class in 1892, followed by Birmingham, Bradford, Bristol and Brighton. Other schools continued to use the standard O class for children who were not able to keep to the required standards, and a London School Board Inspector noted in 1897 that 'of every 70 children in standard I twenty-five are almost entirely ignorant, they misbehaved, learned nothing or truanted' (quoted in Pritchard, 1963, p. 117).

Thus, while doctors and teachers in normal schools were in agreement that special schools were necessary to allow normal schools to proceed smoothly, they were in conflict over who should be in charge of selection procedures. Dr Kerr, a Bradford MO, was of the opinion that if teachers in ordinary schools were allowed to select children for special instruction, they would attempt to get rid of all their dull children. Educationalists, at this time, made no effort to count numbers of possible defective children, whereas a medical man, Dr Warner, undertook several surveys of the incidence of feeble-mindedness and thus enhanced medical claims to dominate selection procedures. His survey of children in Poor Law Schools was used in the Poor Law School Committee Report of 1896 as evidence of a need for special schools and shortly after this report the Interdepartmental Committee on Defective and Epileptic Children, chaired by an HMI, the Rev. T. Sharpe, was convened.

This committee consisted of two doctors, two educationalists and a representative from the Charity Organisation Society; and medical influence on the assessment of children requiring special education emerged paramount from the recommendations of this committee, published in 1898. The one teacher on the committee was overruled on the importance of teacher opinion on selection procedures and the committee concluded that the selection of children for special schools should be medical. The committee preferred the use of the term 'educable defective' to 'feeble-minded' and the children were to be those 'not being imbecile who cannot properly be taught in ordinary schools by ordinary methods'. Epileptic children were to attend ordinary schools only if attacks were more than a month apart. Head teachers or inspectors should make a preliminary selection of children for special schooling to be examined if a doctor and parents should be allowed to attend the examination. A grant should be payable for children in special schools from central funds, providing the child received six hours of manual instruction per week. The recommendations of the committee were put into effect by the passing of the 1899 Elementary Education (Defective and Epileptic Children) Act, but it was an enabling act, not a compulsory one. The familiar contradiction that while defective children should be educated separately, it should not cost too much became evident during the passage of this act. The Chancellor of the Exchequer himself expressed fears that too many local authorities 'especially in Ireland' would discover too many defective children.

By the end of the nineteenth century, a variety of interests were being served by the development of state special education. Economic interests were being served by the manual and trade training emphasised at all schools and institutions for defective children. The transfer of handicapped and defective children out of ordinary education meant that the preparation of a normal productive workforce was not interfered with. Costs were to be kept as low as possible in state special schools and voluntary provision was to be encouraged to lessen the expense of state provision.

The interests of political ruling groups were being served by the placement in separate schools and institutions, of children who might eventually prove troublesome to society, given the assumed links between defect, crime and unemployment. Medical interests were supreme in that doctors had control of selection and assessment procedures for special education, but the interests of educationalists in normal schools were served by the removal of troublesome children. The social origins of state special education can certainly be traced to the desire of educators in normal schools to separate out the defective and the troublesome, and thus special education can be regarded as a safety-valve, allowing the smoother development of the normal education system.

Special education 1900–44

In the early twentieth century there was a move towards the greater segregation of defective children from the normal school system, concentrating particularly on those children considered to be mentally defective. The assumption that the lower social classes were most likely to produce defective children became more pronounced, particularly when the influence of the eugenics movement led to political anxiety that defective children were a danger to society, and 'defect' was linked to moral depravity, crime, pauperism, unemployment and prostitution.

The Royal Commission on the Care and Control of the Feeble-Minded, reporting in 1908, were in no doubt that permanent institutional care was the means to establish continuous control over the feeble-minded, and the establishment of industrial 'colonies' with schools was advocated (*Report of the Royal Commission on the Care and Control of the Feeble-Minded*, 1908, vol. 8, p. 116).

However, since children suitable for the first schools for special instruction, set up during the 1890s, had only been sought in working-class elementary schools, it was inevitable that the first special school children were almost entirely working-class. Eugenic fears were intensified by the development of mental testing (Binet and Simon, 1914), and the acceptance of the notion of fixed, innate intelligence which could not be improved upon.

Political interest in the social control of defective children was therefore paramount in the early twentieth century. A committee on physical deterioration published a report in 1904 and recommended the establishment of special schools in the country for delicate children. Medical interests were served by one recommendation of this committee, that the medical inspection of all children be a duty of all school authorities, and in 1907 the School Medical Service was set up. A clause in the 1918 Education Act required local education authorities to provide for physically handicapped children and by 1919 there were 'schools for delicate children, day and residential schools for cripples, schools in convalescent homes, trade schools, orthopaedic and T.B. hospital schools' (Pritchard, 1963, p. 165).

But political anxiety concerning mental defectives, plus worry that their education might be financially unjustified if their labour was not subsequently used, led to the setting up of a Royal Commission on the Care and Control of the Feeble-Minded in 1904. The Commission, chaired by the Earl of Radnor, included three doctors, two lawyers, the chairman of the eugenics-influenced National Association for Promoting the Welfare of the Feeble-Minded, which had been established in 1896, and the Secretary of the Charity Organisation Society. They were concerned about 'the numbers of mentally defective persons whose training is neglected, over whom no sufficient control is exercised and whose wayward and irresponsible lives are productive of crime and misery . . . and of much continuous expenditure wasteful to the community' (*Report of the Royal Commission on the Care and Control of the Feeble-Minded*, 1908).

The Royal Commission was not impressed by educational arrangements for defective children: 'we find a local and permissive system of education which is available here and there for a limited section of mentally defective children . . . which is supplemented by no supervision and control and is in consequence often misdirected' (vol. 8, p. 1).

The working-class parents of defective children were singled out for condemnation: 'The ignorance and want of foresight of the parent is very great – they constantly refuse offers of industrial training, and will not forgo even small earnings to gain possible future efficiency' (vol. 8, p. 96).

The emphasis of the report was on the control and direction of children who had been through special schooling, economic control was directed towards making the children self-sufficient, and the possible waste of resources in educating even 'dull and backward' children was stressed. Dr Kerr, the London County Council medical officer, gave evidence to the Commission that as far as dull children were concerned: 'Years of school work seem a wasted outlay, . . . if they could be separated effectively at the age of ten or twelve, a training to become hewers of wood and drawers of water might make them happier and more useful to others' (vol. 8, p. 99).

Estimates of the 'success' of special schooling was rated by the Commission in terms of economic self-sufficiency and social control: 'whether the number of those who, when they left school, could materially support themselves were few or many it [special schooling] helped to make the larger number of children cleaner in person and habits, more orderly and more moral' (vol. 8, p. 103).

A major recommendation of the Royal Commission was that the responsibility for the education of mentally defective children be moved from education authorities to a new, medically dominated, Board of Control. The recommendations of the Royal Commission represented the high point of medical domination for assessing defective children. If the care of all defective children had indeed passed to the Board of Control a whole new medically dominated bureaucracy would have developed with far-reaching consequences for all 'subnormal' children. However, educational interests began to challenge medical interests and not all the recommendations of the Royal Commission found their way into the 1913 Mental Deficiency Act. In the intervening years, educationalists had had time to realise that their own interests lay in retaining control of as many children as possible in education and 175 school authorities had made some provision by the time that the 1914 Education (Defective and Epileptic

Children) Act made the 1899 provisions compulsory. Education authorities now had the duty of ascertaining which children were defective, and, of these, which children were incapable of education in special schools. Only these latter children were passed to local Mental Deficiency Committees, responsible to a Board of Control.

In addition to the interests of educational administrators in retaining educational control of as many children as possible, and the interests of normal schools in functioning without defective children, a third educational vested interest was provided by special school teachers, who had formed a professional association with its own journal in 1903, and had developed skills and competencies in dealing with defective children. These teachers needed to be sure that their clients would, in fact, attend special schools, by now stigmatised by association with a variety of social ills, and the 1914 Education Act contained a clause enabling local authorities to compel parents to send their children into special schooling. This 'certification procedure' did nothing to reduce the stigma attached to special school attendance. By the early 1920s, the stigmatisation of defective children had, historically, reached its most pronounced point and subsequently efforts have been made to reduce the stigma and blur the more overt control function of special education.

By the 1920s, medical officers were anxious to consolidate their new area of competence and in 1921 the Medical Branch of the Board of Education was given powers to inspect special schools. But the new profession of psychology was seeking a foothold in assessment procedures for special schooling, as the rise of the mental testing movement had been closely bound up with measuring subnormality. Psychologists, through mental testing procedures, were acquiring the power to legitimate the removal of large numbers of children from normal education. The charismatic figure who represented psychological interests was Cyril Burt, appointed as the first psychologist to the London County Council in 1913. He was the first psychologist to use 'mental' tests to ascertain children for special schools, while working on the construction and standardisation of tests (Burt, 1921).

Burt was a member of a committee set up jointly by the Board of Education and the Board of Control in 1924 to inquire into 'mental defect'. Four members of this committee were medical officers, and two were in the Medical Branch of the Board of Education. One head of a colony school was on the committee, but otherwise teachers were not represented. The committee relied heavily on the report of an inquiry by Dr Lewis into the incidence of subnormal children in England. Lewis encapsulated all vested interests in one person. He was a medical doctor, had worked as a teacher and lectured in educational psychology. The findings of his inquiry served all interests, but particularly psychological interests, as he administered group intelligence tests, standardised by Cyril Burt, to decide whether children selected by teachers from their classes were or were not feeble-minded.

The Wood Committee reported in 1929, and urged that the educable defective child be merged with children regarded as dull and backward and be envisaged as a single group presenting a single educational and administrative problem (Wood, 1929). They recommended the abolition of certification procedures, and urged that special schools be presented to parents as a 'helpful variant' of normal education. Given the stigmatisation of special schooling by the influence of eugenicists, the linkage of defect to social and moral depravity, and the certification procedures, it was not surprising that parents were unenthusiastic. A major problem facing educational interests since this time has been to find a legitimating ideology by which special schooling can be regarded as 'helpful'. The National Union of Teachers was opposed to the abolition of certification, teachers in special schools were not anxious to lose their clients and they were of the opinion that without compulsion parents would not send their children to special schools. However, the interests of special educators, along with a variety of other educational interests, were considerably furthered by the 1944 Education Act and post-war development.

Special education 1944–70

The 1944 Education Act and subsequent Ministry of Education regulations concerning special education can be regarded as a major effort by educationalists to move as many 'defective' children as possible out of medical domination and place them firmly under an educational aegis. Local education authorities were required to meet the needs of handicapped children in the form of special educational treatment within their general duty, to provide primary and secondary schools.

A new set of categories for children requiring special education was worked out, the number of categories increasing from four to eleven. Partially sighted and partially hearing children were separated from blind and deaf, delicate, diabetic, epileptic and physically handicapped formed four separate categories, educable defective children became educationally subnormal, and two new categories, speech defect and maladjusted, were created. Maladjusted children had already become important clients, enhancing the prestige of psychologists and the developing child guidance movement, twenty-two child guidance clinics being recognised as part of the school medical service by 1939. Diabetic and delicate children were linked in 1953. This expansion of categories is not surprising, considering that for the first time England and Wales were about to develop a co-ordinated system of compulsory, mass primary and secondary education. Central and local education authorities, having experienced the problems particular groups of children had posed after the introduction of mass primary education, allowed no chance for secondary education to be similarly upset. To develop a workable system it was essential to exclude as many children as possible who might obstruct or inconvenience the smooth running of the normal schools, hence the need for careful categorisation. In addition, the 1944 Act allowed for a tripartite system of secondary schooling by 'age, aptitude and ability'. Selection by 'ability' sanctioned selected by 'disability'. Thus, the duty was laid upon local authorities to arrange provision for pupils suffering from 'any disability of body or mind'. This requirement was vague and general enough to incorporate all children who might conceivably upset normal education.

However, the requirements of the act did conflict with the egalitarian ideology which became more pronounced after the war; also, provision for such a wide variety of 'disability' was undoubtedly immediately seen to be expensive. The loophole to accommodate this was that less seriously handicapped children could be educated in ordinary schools, either 'normally' or in special classes. But suggestions that children in need of special

education could remain in ordinary schools immediately conflicted with two educational interests: the goal of removing the
children so that the normal schools could function efficiently
would be frustrated, and the expanding profession of 'special'
education would lose clients. Thus, it was not surprising that
provision for special education failed to develop in ordinary
schools to any extent. As the 1946 Ministry of Education
guidelines put it: 'anyone who has known children in any of the
categories will agree that the varieties of education offered in
ordinary primary and secondary schools do not meet their needs'
(Ministry of Education, 1946). After 1945, children not considered to be capable of education were passed to the health
authorities and became categorised 'as severely subnormal', and,
despite the rhetoric of 'help' and 'needs', it was firmly recognised
that some parents, particularly of the ESN, would need coercing
into accepting that their children would be excluded from normal
education – a certificate signed by a doctor could be used to
coerce unwilling parents.

Thus the handicapped pupils' form 1 was used to secure compulsory attendance at a special school. This compulsion made
nonsense of the idea of providing special education in ordinary
school, to threaten one child with compulsory attendance while
allowing another to remain in ordinary school was a manifest
contradiction. Many LEAs have subsequently insisted that they
do not use the 'formal procedure' of HP1 but there has always
been some confusion over what exactly constituted 'formal procedures' (Ministry of Education, 1961; Brindle, 1973).

After the war, special educational treatment came to be associated with provision in separate schools, with only medical officers
given statutory powers in the assessment procedures, under the
1944 Act. However, mental testing had become a part of the
procedures and psychological as well as medical and educational
interests were served by the expansion in special education.
Other professional interests also expanded; the Underwood
Committee on Maladjusted Children (1955) had recommended
an integrated child guidance service, in which psychiatrists, social
workers and others would be involved, as well as medical officers
and psychologists, and the Quirk Committee (1972) recommended an expanded speech therapy service and the establishment of a professional organisation. The category which

expanded most, after the war, was that of educational subnormality. As the Warnock Report put it: 'the needs of the E.S.N. remained obstinately unsatisfied in spite of continuous expansion since 1945' (*Special Education Needs . . .*, p. 23).

The number of children in ESN schools doubled between 1947 and 1955 (from 12,060 to 22,639 – with a further 27,000 awaiting placement), and over two-thirds of referrals of 'handicapped' children in the 1960s were for (mild) educational subnormality. From a sociological perspective, what was happening was that teachers in ordinary schools were taking full advantage of the deliberately vague and complex definitions of an 'ESN' child, and were using the category for the purpose of removing children who were troublesome in both learning and behavioural terms. They preferred this category to the maladjusted category and there were few maladjusted schools available. The Ministry of Education acknowledged the situation in 1955: 'it has become less difficult to place the really troublesome educationally sub-normal boy or girl, whose mental disability is compounded by behavioural difficulties and perhaps a record of delinquency' (Ministry of Education, 1956).

Special education 1970–80

The history of special education during the 1970s can be interpreted as continued conflicts of professional interests and ideologies, but economic interests are, as always, underlying arguments about resources and provision, and about the work potential of the handicapped. Political interests in the control of potentially disruptive groups of children via special education were also dramatically extended in this decade.

The interests of special educators appeared to lie in further careful categorisation of children considered to have special needs. At an international conference of special educators (London, 1966) the presidential address suggested that aphasic children (children not deaf but with communication difficulties), dyslexic children (those whose difficulty lay in interpreting the printed character), autistic children (those 'unable to tune in to ordinary human wavelengths'), psychiatrically crippled children (those stressed by conditions in modern cities), and socially handicapped children (presumably the children of the poor) should all be recognised as distinct categories. Yet at the same time, egalitarian distaste for segregating certain groups of children, plus the expense in providing for a growing number of 'handicapped' in special schools, had led to an intensified debate on 'integration', or provision in ordinary schools for children formerly categorised out of the schools.

The interests of educators, particularly the now considerable bureaucracy concerned with special education, were dominant over medical interests when in 1970 children who had been termed uneducable mental defectives until 1944 and 'severely subnormal' after 1959, were integrated into special education. The Mental Health Act of 1959 had recommended that these children should receive education and training, but in 1970, by the Education (Handicapped Children) Act, these children were formally brought within the education system. Section 57 of the 1944 Act, whereby uneducable children were the responsibility of the Health Service, was repealed and the children were placed under the local education authority. About 32,750 children were involved who had previously been catered for in training units, hospitals and special care units. They were children with severe and often multiple defects. The Department of Education and Science, in a report on *The Last to Come In*, were enthusiastic about the integration of formerly mentally handicapped children with educationally subnormal children. The severely handicapped were to be known as ESN-S (severe) in contrast to ESN-M (mild). The report noted that 'the inclusion of mentally handicapped children in the category E.S.N. gives recognition to the fact that mental handicap is a continuum'.

This notion of a continuum of defect had been developing alongside the historical attempts to impose administrative and legal classification on subnormality in hierarchical grades. Various reports had acknowledged the artifice of rigid distinctions, and then proceeded to define arbitrary categories. Younghusband (1970) had suggested reworking the categories of handicap, and the inclusions of a category of 'multiple handicap'. This concept has been used as a reason for the abolition of all categories: 'the present form of categorisation assumes that all handicapped children have only a single disability, whereas many have more than one' (DES, 1980b).

A DES report on special education in April 1973 purported to be *A Fresh Look* at the situation. The report deplored the use of statutory categories of handicap, but there was no suggestion at that time that the statutory categories be removed. Instead, five authorities were recruited to pilot a 'descriptive list based on education needs' alongside the statutory categories. 1973 was also the year that a committee to review educational provisions and for handicapped children and young people was set up under the chairmanship of Mrs Mary Warnock. By 1975 the DES had prepared a circular designed 'to clear up uncertainties and confusion which surround the subject of ascertainment, and to provide a fresh statement of what is involved in discovering which children require special education, and in recommending what form it should take'.

The implications of Circular 2/75 are clearly that the DES considers an educational model of assessing children in need of special education to be preferable to a medical model. However, the educational model envisaged is heavily oriented towards an educational-psychological assessment. The DES had, since 1944, made statements to the effect that decisions should be educational; the medical officer had been retained as the only statutory decision-maker via section 34 of the 1944 Act. In the Circular, nineteen years after the inception of Form HP 1 – 'the prescribed certificate' for children whose parents object to their 'treatment' at special schools – the DES did criticise the Form as having gone further than section 34 required 'by calling on the Medical Officer to make what are really educational judgements'.

However, Circular 2/75 not only retains the 'certificate' to be signed by a doctor, but also requires that all assessments of children for special education be notified to their own GP. The circular introduced new forms in place of the handicapped pupil (HP) form, as 'standard' forms are still desirable in the interests of handicapped children moving from one area to another and 'to ensure that the insights of doctor, educational psychologist and teacher' are made available when children are being considered for special education. The new 'special education' (SE) forms 1–3 are intended to replace HP forms 2–4.

SE1 is for completion by a teacher or head concerning a child who may require special education, SE2 is for completion by a medical officer, SE3 by a psychologist and SE4, a new 'summary' form, was to be completed by a psychologist or LEA advisor.

In 1976, motivated primarily by egalitarian ideologies, the Labour government decided to incorporate a section on special education into the 1976 Education Act, an act designed primarily to enforce comprehensivisation in all areas of England and Wales. The relevant section, section 10, substituted for section 33 (ii) of the 1944 Act, a clause which was intended to change the legal emphasis from special educational treatment in special schools, to the provision of special education, for all categories of handicapped children, in ordinary county and voluntary schools. Section 10 laid down that pupils shall be educated in special schools only if they cannot be given efficient instruction in ordinary schools, or if the cost of instruction in ordinary schools would cause 'unreasonable public expenditures'.

Section 10 was never implemented and the Conservative government decided not to implement it, on the economic grounds that 'in present economic circumstances there is no possibility of finding the massive additional resources . . . which would be required to enable every ordinary school to provide an adequate education for children with serious educational difficulties' (DES, 1980b).

The major event in special education in the 1970s was undoubtedly the publication of the report of the Committee of Enquiry into the education of handicapped children and young people (the Warnock Report) in 1978. The variety of professionals on this committee indicates the expansion of vested interests in the, by now, considerable field of special education. Administrators, doctors, psychologists, heads of special schools, social service directors, university professors, a retired NUT secretary, and a TUC secretary were represented on the committee. One parent of handicapped children was on the committee but she was also chairman of the education committee of the National Deaf Children's Society. One head of an ordinary school was a member.

There are many similarities between the Warnock Report and the Wood Report of 1929. Both Reports attempted to present special education as a helpful variant of normal education, deploring the stigma attached to special schooling, while at the same time recommending an expansion of special education, and a re-working of categories. In the Warnock Report, the expansion of special schooling was to extend to one child in five, or 20 per cent of the school population who at some time during their school career would need 'some form of special educational treatment'. The abolition of statutory categories of handicap was recommended in favour of a 'broader concept of special educational need', but descriptive labels were to be attached to children. A non-statutory category of 'child with learning difficulty' was suggested, to embrace the current educationally subnormal children and children classed as remedial in normal schools. As the majority of these children are of manual working-class parentage, this important sociological point will be taken up in the next chapter. The recommendation that children who had been placed, on an *ad hoc* basis, in a variety of units and centres for disruptive children during the 1970s should now officially come within special education, will provide a further safety-valve for normal education to function unimpeded by troublesome children.

The ten types of special school provision envisaged by the Warnock Committee are as follows (*Special Educational Needs . . .*, 1978, p. 96):

(i) Full-time education in an ordinary class with any necessary help and support.

(ii) Education in an ordinary class with periods of withdrawal to a special class or unit.

(iii) Education in a special class or unit with periods of attendance at an ordinary class, and full involvement in the general community life and extra-curriculum activities of the schools.

(iv) Full-time education in a special class or unit with social contact with the main school.

(v) Education in a special school (day or residential) with some lessons at a neighbouring ordinary school.

(vi) Full-time education in a day special school with social contact with an ordinary school.

(vii) Full-time education in a residential special school with social contacts with an ordinary school.

(viii) Short-term education in hospital or other establishment.

(ix) Long-term education as in (viii).

(x) Home tuition.

This suggested variety of possibilities illustrates the recognition of the many educational interests involved in classifying children out of normal education.

The 1980 White Paper on *Special Needs in Education*, which formed the basis for new legislation, began by noting that the Warnock Report 'is a landmark in the development of policy and practice in this important area'. The concept of 'special educational needs', as described in the Warnock Report, has been accepted as a basis for legislation, and statutory categories of handicap are to be abolished. Economic interests, however, dictate that there will be no widespread 'integration' of children who are currently assessed out of the normal system back into it, for as one commentator has noted: 'the three words that appear most often in the White Paper . . . are not . . . special educational needs, they are Present Economic Circumstances' *(The Times Educational Supplement*, 8 August 1980). Professional interests will be catered for by more complex procedures for assessing, recording and reviewing children with special educational needs. The sociological implications of the moves to dismantle a complex sub-system of the education system that has been built up over 100 years will be examined in the next chapter.

This chapter has sought to demonstrate that the history of the expansion of special education over the last hundred years can be looked at from an alternative perspective to the humanitarian view of 'doing good' to children. Sociologists are usually suspicious when one group claims to be doing good to other groups, particularly when legal coercion is involved. A sociological perspective on the history of special education can show how provision developed to cater for the needs of ordinary schools, the interests of the wider industrial society and the specific interests of professionals.

Chapter Three · **Issues and dilemmas in special education**

Heated debates about educational issues, as Broadfoot has noted (1979), often do more to obscure than to clarify the real issues. However, the previous chapter's discussion of the development of special education in terms of conflicting interests and wider social needs, rather than in terms of humanitarian evolution, should make it clear that some groups concerned with special education actually have vested interests in structuring debates in particular ways rather than clarifying issues. The debate on integration provides a good example. It is to be expected that special school teachers would like to structure the debate in terms of the difficulties inherent in the integration of handicapped children into ordinary school life if this would eventually lose them clients. Administrators, on the other hand, might like to structure the debate in terms of which form of education costs less. This chapter examines what have emerged as some of the important issues and dilemmas in special education: categorisation and selection, the rhetoric of special needs, and the integration debate. These issues are often presented in purely 'educational' terms, whereas they actually reflect wider social, political and professional interests of various groups.

Categorisation

The terminology employed in special education to describe and categorise children is complex and ever-changing. This is not accidental, it is the result of the competing interests involved. Spectre and Kitsuse (1977) have pointed out that where there is competition between groups who have vested interests in defining weaker social groups, the labels and definitions finally applied are those of the winning group. Thus early medical interests in special education meant that doctors had an interest in making as many of the categories as possible medically oriented, while educational interests sought to make categories educational if possible. Medical claims to diagnose 'feeble-mindedness' were not fully routed until the publication of Circular 2/75, which stated firmly that whether and where a child needed special education was primarily an educational, not medical, matter.

The medical terminology of defect and disability did dominate until the 1944 Education Act, when defect was redefined in terms of handicap, although it was to be 'children suffering from a defect of body or mind' who were to be discovered by local education authorities. Table 3.1 illustrates the historical development of categories, and notes some categories which have at times been suggested, which were never statutorily adopted. It is interesting to observe that in just over fifty years, from 1893 to 1945, two 'educational' categories of handicap became eleven. The handicapped pupils regulations, published in 1945, to describe the categories (Ministry of Education, 1945) did demonstrate that educational administrative influence had triumphed over medical influence, although the professional skills and mystiques of medical personnel were to be used to legitimate the placing of children in the categories. The administrative logic of extended classification by categories in 1945 was underpinned by prevalent psychological conceptions of 'handicap' as a static entity, with mental capacities as fixed and innate, and, since the 1944 Education Act was enshrining the notion of selection by differentiation, with children being assigned to secondary school by age, aptitude and ability, it would have seemed rational at that time to categorise by handicap and assign children to separate schools. This also fitted in with the need, noted in chapter 2, to provide a rationalisation for the removal of extended numbers of troublesome children from secondary, as well as primary, education in 1945.

However, administrative problems over the static nature of the categories, in addition to changing post-war ideologies, meant that the categorisation of children soon became unsatisfactory. Economic pressures were important – it was financially impossible for every local authority to set up schools for all categories of handicap, and provision over the whole country developed in a patchy manner. The efforts of various groups to extend the educational recognition of categories of handicap was resisted by the administration. For example, medical pressure to add autistic children to the official list of statutory handicaps (Eden, 1976) and the effort of pressure groups to have dyslexia recognised as an educational handicap, were frustrated, although these two conditions were officially recognised to exist under the 1970 Chronically Sick and Disabled Persons Act. On the other hand, Stott's 'inconsequential child' (Stott, 1966) never became recognised.

The problematic nature of categorisation can be illustrated at this point by a consideration of development of the category of educational subnormality and of the non-statutory category of a disruptive child. The first guidelines on ESN were laid down in the 1946 pamphlet (Ministry of Education, 1946). In this document, educational retardation was noted as being caused by 'limited ability' or by 'other considerations' or by both together. Limited ability was considered, on the basis of then current psychological knowledge, to have a genetic basis and was likely to be permanent, although special schools were thought to play a useful part in training the children. The ministry guidelines were based in a large part on Cyril Burt's work on *The Backward Child* (Burt, 1937; Hearnshaw, 1979). Thus, two groups of children were explicitly identified here – the innately dull, and the backward – but LEAs were told that it was not necessary to make separate arrangements for the two sets of children. 'One of the advantages of the new Act is that no decision as to the cause of retardation may be given before the child is given special educational treatment' (Ministry of Education, 1946).

Thus, every retarded child was potentially ESN and the cause need not be taken into account. As a rough guideline to how many children and which children should be classed as ESN the pamphlet spoke of a 'large body of opinion' who favoured giving special educational treatment 'If the child is so retarded that his standard of work is below that achieved by a child 20 per cent younger than he is'. An IQ of 55 was suggested as a cut-off point at which a child cannot be educated in a special school and teachers were urged not to be sentimental over referring 'detrimental or low-grade' children to the mental health authorities. ESN pupils were to be children with IQs of between 55 and 70–75 who were of

Table 3.1 Statutory categories of handicap 1886–1981

Statutory categories						Suggested descriptive categories
1886	1899	1913	1945	1962	1970	1981
Idiot	Idiot	Idiot	Severely sub-normal (SSN)	Severely sub-normal (SSN)	Educationally subnormal (severe)	Child with learning difficulties (severe)
Imbecile	Imbecile	Imbecile				
		Moral imbecile		Psychopathic		
	Blind	Blind	Blind		Blind	Blind
			Partially sighted		Partially sighted	Partially sighted
	Deaf	Deaf	Deaf		Deaf	Deaf
			Partially deaf	Partial hearing	Partial hearing	Partial hearing
	Epileptic	Epileptic	Epileptic		Epileptic	Epileptic
	Defective	Mental defective (feeble-minded)	Educationally subnormal		Educationally subnormal (mild or moderate)	Child with learning difficulty (mild or moderate)
			Maladjusted	Maladjusted	Maladjusted	Maladjusted disruptive
		Physical defective	Physically handicapped		Physically handicapped	Physically handicapped
			Speech defect		Speech defect	Speech defect
			Delicate	Delicate	Delicate	Delicate
			Diabetic			
						Dyslexic? Autistic?

Special Educational Needs (spanning the 1981 column)

Note Categories suggested but never adopted include: the neuropathic child, the inconsequential child, the psychiatrically crippled child, the aphasic child and others. Autism and dyslexia were recognised under the 1970 Chronically Sick and Disabled Persons Act.

innately low intelligence or functioning at 20 per cent below their age level but without behaviour problems, 8–9 per cent of all registered pupils less seriously retarded 'for other reasons' may be retained in ordinary schools for special educational treatment, but in 'good schools drawing from suburban areas' the proportion of retarded children may be small.

By 1956 the notion of special classes for children in ordinary schools had given way to an acceptance that educationally subnormal children needed help 'which ordinary schools cannot give' (Ministry of Education, 1956). If no guidance was available for educationalists in deciding which children were ESN at this time, the medical officer, who had the duty of making the actual decision on the child, was expected to give a clear decision. Section 15(a) of Form 2 HP (report on a child examined for a disability of mind) required the medical officer to state that in his opinion 'the child is/is not educationally sub-normal'. A 1961 circular, one of a number of attempts in the 1960s and early 1970s to further define educationally sub-normal children, noted that ESN children include the 'temporarily retarded as well as the innately dull, who may suitably receive some or all of their special education in ordinary schools as well as those who need to attend special schools' (Ministry of Education, 1961).

A 1972 definition encapsulated a series of contradictions, noting that

> educationally sub-normal pupils include both children who are educationally backward, (that is, their attainments are appreciably less than those of average children of the same age) whether or not they are mentally retarded, and also children of average and above average ability who for various reasons are educationally retarded, that is their attainments are not commensurate with their ability. (Department of Education and Science, 1972)

The 1946 notion that children can be backward for 'other conditions' persisted in the 1972 notion of backwardness for 'various reasons'. The deliberate policy of not tracing 'causes' of educational backwardness while implicitly attributing it to environmental and family deficiency has been noticeable from the 1946 pamphlet to the 1978 Report of the Warnock Committee.

By this time a child could be educationally backward with a high or low IQ; he or she could be ESN without requiring special schooling, or could be of above average ability and still require special schooling. No cause need be established for a child's retardation, but teachers were expected to distinguish different degrees and types of backwardness. Special education was not to be looked on as a form of education peculiar to special schools, but children could be certified as requiring special schooling. Definitions of educational subnormality were supposed to be educational, but only medical officers had any statutory powers in the ascertainment procedures. An ESN child may or may not be distinguished from a backward child who may remain in ordinary school. In the 1940s he or she was not initially intended to be a troublesome child, but troublesome children had tended to be referred as potentially ESN. Formal ascertainment procedures were to be used sparingly, but there was confusion over what exactly constituted a formal procedure.

No research throughout this period, 1947–70, had attempted to find out nationally what ESN schools were doing in terms of goals, organisation or curriculum. One point that does emerge clearly is that the optimistic view that a large group of children had had their educational needs catered for – the humanitarian perspective – had little justification. With no criteria as to how teachers should define an educational need, and with the legal designation of an ESN child being the responsibility of a medical officer, it is difficult to see how children were being defined on the basis of educational need. The most one could say was that a set of procedures had been developed which isolated a particular group of children into separate schools, the major characteristic of these children throughout the one-hundred-year period discussed here being that they were predominantly the children of semi- or unskilled manual working-class people.

The crucial category, which developed on an *ad hoc* basis during the 1970s, was that of 'disruptive' pupils. An HMI survey of the variety of centres, units and classes for behaviourally troublesome pupils, undertaken in 1977, showed that 69 out of 96 LEAs in England had established such units, 1974 being a peak year for establishment. They reported that 239 units were catering for 3,962 pupils (Department of Education and Science, 1978). However, an Advisory Council for Education Survey in 1979 discovered 386 units serving 5,857 pupils (Advisory Council for Education, 1980). The establishment of this unofficial category of special education was legally based on section 56 of the 1944 Education Act which allowed LEAs to make provision for children 'otherwise than at school', but during the 1970s it rapidly became an alternative to the referral of troublesome children as potentially ESN-M or maladjusted. Official special education required a lengthy assessment procedure, disruptive units could accommodate children immediately. One commentator on the development of these units linked them firmly with the interests of special educators:

> If there did not exist such a powerful special schools lobby, would any LEA have been able to get away with initiating this whole new sin-bin section of special education, with even less formal procedures and safeguards than the existing and still expanding special education section? (Newell, 1980)

The expedient solution to the problem of the continual creation of new categories of handicap has been the substitution of the notion of special education needs as a rationalisation for special education. New legislation will remove statutory categories of handicap and 'special needs' will become the legitimating terminology by which up to a fifth of children may be removed from normal education. The recommendations of the Warnock Report suggested that descriptive labels should remain and children should still be described as blind, deaf, and so on. It was suggested that children currently classed as remedial in normal schooling would join those currently ascertained as ESN – the whole to be known as Children with Learning Difficulties – mild, moderate or severe. The Report recommended that the descriptive category of maladjustment should also remain, although the National Council for Special Education has suggested the label 'children with adjustment difficulties' (NCSE, 1979). It is interesting to note in Table 3.2 that the numbers of children categorised as maladjusted in 1979, 22,402, has increased from 6,000 in 1974 – 1974 appears to have been a crucial year in terms of teacher tolerance of behaviour problems in normal schools.

Table 3.2 records the numbers of children ascertained by LEAs

Table 3.2 Numbers of children ascertained as requiring special education in 1979

Blind	1,168	Handicapped children	
Partially sighted	2,819	in non-maintained	
Deaf	4,115	approval special	
Partially hearing	7,256	schools	8,297
Physically handicapped	16,677		
Delicate	6,893	Handicapped children	
Epileptic	1,689	in independent	
Speech defect	2,972	schools	7,477
ESN	119,005		
Maladjusted	22,402		

Source: Adopted from DES *Statistics in Education 1979*.

as requiring special educational treatment in 1979. It is not broken down by sex, but it is important to record that in the crucial 'non-normative' categories of ESN and maladjusted, boys out-number girls by three to one.

Normative and non-normative categories

The major sociological interest in the categories of special educa-tion lies in the conflation of *normative* with *non-normative* condi-tions. Although, as noted in chapter 1, there could even be debate over what constitutes deafness, there can be some normative agreement about the existence of certain categories of handicap, or special need, particularly those which fall into what is currently defined as a medical sphere of competence. Thus blind, deaf, epileptic, physical handicaps, speech defects and severe types of mental handicap could all arguably be normatively agreed upon by most people – professional or lay people, using common-sense but often medical assumptions as well as professional expertise. On the other hand, the categories of feeble-minded, education-ally subnormal, maladjusted and disruptive are not, and never will be, normative categories. There are no adequate measuring instruments or agreed criteria in the social world to decide upon these particular categories, whether descriptive or statutory.

There can be, and is, legitimate argument between professionals, parents, other interested groups and the general public, over what constitutes these categories. The answer to the question 'what is' an ESN-M child or a maladjusted child will depend more upon the values, beliefs and interests of those making the judgments than on any qualities intrinsic to the child. Kennedy recently pointed out that 'What is the normal state against which to measure abnormalities is a product of social and cultural values and expectations' (Kennedy, 1980). The following case study may illustrate this point.

Daren O. was referred in 1975 at age eight for educational and disruptive reasons. He came from the infants school as a non-reader, and the head said he 'had time off school to look after the babies at home'. Also 'he is often aggressive . . . in P.E. he is often removed from these lessons until he has calmed down'. The psychologist gave his IQ as 67 and wrote that 'his attainments place him firmly in the ESN range'. The psychologist also noted white pigmentation on the boy's lips, 'he looks like a minstrel – poor lad!' The SCMO also recommended ESN schooling and noted that 'he presented an odd-looking boy with puffy eyes and leucoderma skin on lips'. His mother is bringing up six children while her husband is serving a prison sentence. She came from Jamaica to work in a factory in 1962, married and had her children in England. She had a nervous breakdown and the children were temporarily in care and she said she missed Daren the most. She has a younger boy at deaf school, and had been 'persuaded' by the psychologist to let Daren go to ESN school on condition that he did not go to the local ESN school as 'his friends would call him names'. The head of the school to which he did go said 'mother didn't want him to go to the barmy school on her patch'. After visiting the school, Mrs O. thought Daren got good special help, but she wanted him to go back to normal school at eleven. 'They told me that if he makes enough progress to satisfy the education committee he can go back . . . I don't want him at that [ESN] school until he's 16' (Tomlinson, 1981).

The judgments of the professionals about this child are based on a variety of beliefs about the social and racial characteristics of the child and family. The judgments could legitimately be called into question, and there can be little normative agreement as to placement in the ESN-M category.

From the point of view of normal schools, the one way in which conflation of normative and non-normative categories becomes possible is through the recognition that all the children are, in the widest possible sense, potentially 'troublesome', and we are brought back to reiterating the point that special schooling functions as a safety-valve for normal education, by removing troublesome children. There is no educational argument for the continued conflation of normative and non-normative categories. The new legislation based on the notion of special needs is likely to intensify the confusion of normative categories with non-normative, and from a sociological point of view it becomes very important to ask what sort of children, in terms of social class and background, are being selected for the non-normative categories, whether they are statutory or merely descriptive.

Selection and the social problem classes

Debates about the nature of the education system as a system of social selection in a class-stratified society have been pursued for some time in the sociology of education (see Karabel and Halsey, 1977). The two major theoretical perspectives concerned to explain educational selection procedures and their relationship to society are the functionalist view, which assumes a consensus in society, and the perspective informed by models of social conflict and control. From the technical-functionalist perspective, education is seen as the mechanism which sorts people out into occupational roles. When the society becomes technically more complex, more complex sorting procedures are required. This view is supported by the liberal-reformist ideology (Broadfoot, 1979) which assumed that education is a 'good' available to everyone in a just society according to his/her abilities. This notion was written into the Warnock Report, which, in making out a case for the education of all children, noted that 'education as we conceive it, is a good . . . to which all human beings are entitled' (*Special Educational Needs* . . ., 1978, p. 6). Careful assessment procedures have been developed to sort people out, at both the bright and the 'dull or handicapped' end of the ability spectrum.

The selection of children for special education *appears* to be based on 'natural' inequalities so self-evident that even conflict-oriented sociologists have seldom questioned the naturalness, and the notion that certain children should naturally be categorised out of the normal education system fitted in very well with a functionalist view of society. Pritchard, for example, was of the opinion that the increase in the numbers of handicapped children in the twentieth century was because more were unable to cope with higher social and technical demands made upon them (Pritchard, 1963). On the other hand, conflict sociologists have located inequalities in the education system and the way children are sorted out in different types of education in terms of the desire of dominant classes to use the system to reproduce their class and maintain order and control among less powerful groups. Procedures for educational selection are seen from this viewpoint as a legitimation for social class reproduction. The education system is considered to have taken over the function of legitimating unequal power, privilege and status relations between social classes (Bowles and Gintis, 1976). The insights of Bourdieu and Passeron, two French sociologists, would appear to provide particular alternative insights into the process of selection for special education and the social uses of some kinds of special education as a means of social control (Bourdieu and Passeron, 1977). Their work is concerned with demonstrating the way the education system legitimates and perpetuates the current social order by making social hierarchies appear to be based on gifts, merits and skills. Educational advancement or exclusion is based on ostensibly fair, meritocratic testing procedures. But they point out that the system demands a cultural competence which it does not itself provide. An advantage is given to families who possess 'cultural capital' and can pass it on to their children. The education system only appears to be based on democratic, just ways of certifying achievement and non-achievement; in their view it is actually more a method of legitimating relationships of social dominance and social control.

Now this kind of conflict perspective does have an appeal as an alternative way of examining who gets selected for special education, particularly for the non-normative categories. An examination of the social class representation in all the categories of handicap demonstrates that, while the normative categories of blind, deaf and so on (the nearest we will get to 'natural' in-equalities) contain children from all social classes, the non-normative categories, the ESN-M, maladjusted and the disrup-tive, contain almost exclusively children from manual working-class parentage. In addition, since the settlement of black immig-rants and their families in Britain, these categories have drawn in a disproportionate number of black children, (ILEA, 1968; Tom-linson, 1981).

It is important to note that the number of children categorised as ESN-M has always added up to half of *all* children classified as handicapped since 1945. The criteria for classifying children into this category have, as we have seen, always been problematic and the type of schooling has long been stigmatised by connections with undesirable social characteristics. From a conflict perspec-tive it would appear that the ESN-M category is more a mechan-ism for moving some troublesome working-class and black chil-dren out of the normal education system than anything else. The social selection of children for special education will become even more biased towards the incorporation of working-class children under the new legislation (Department of Education and Science, 1980b). Remedial and disruptive children, who are not to be offi-cially recognised as part of special education, have always been of predominantly working-class origin (see, for example, Willis, 1977). Special educational provision will in future be much *more* heavily skewed to this sector of the population.

From a conflict perspective much of special education can be regarded as a form of social control over a part of what used to be termed the 'social problem classes' (Burt, 1935; Topliss, 1977). The persistent connection of mild subnormality with the lower working class stemmed particularly from the early 'discovery' of feeble-minded children in the Board Schools in the poorest dis-tricts of London. It was the children of the poor who were troublesome to the state education system. The common-sense assumption that only the lower classes produce dull children was assisted by the ability of upper and middle classes to provide privately for their dull and defective children. This was sporadi-cally acknowledged at the beginning of the century; the 1908 Royal Commission hoped that the 'higher social class – the well-to-do' would 'have their sentiments quickened' to approve of colony schools for their feeble-minded children (*Report of the*

Royal Commission on the Care and Control of the Feeble-Minded, 1908, vol. 8, p. 94). However, the upper and middle class continued to make private provision or deny that they produced such children. Tredgold, in the first edition of his book in 1908, painted a delightful picture of upper-class dullness:

> Throughout the country there are hundreds of feeble-minded persons, many of them gentlefolk by birth . . . they perform little household tasks and outdoor duties, take up simple hobbies like poker-work, stamp collecting and amateur cabinet-making and enter into the ordinary social amusements of their class. (Tredgold, 1908, p. 175)

During the 1920s the influence of the eugenics movement was at its strongest in Britain, and the linkages made between low social class, dullness and social vice had become both expert view and common-sense opinion. The Wood Committee on Mental Deficiency was quite explicit as to the social problem class threatening society.

> In any community a large number of them [defectives] will be found in a restricted group of families. Let us suppose we could segregate as a separate community all the families containing mental defectives. We would find we had collected a most interesting social group . . . a much larger proportion of insane persons, epileptics, paupers, crimimals, unemployables, habitual slum dwellers, prostitutes, inebriates and other social inefficients. The overwhelming majority of the families thus collected would belong to that section of the community we propose to call the social problem class. (Wood Report, 1929, pt 3, p. 80)

Thus, the connection was firmly made between defects and a lack of intelligence, low socio-economic status, and a variety of undesirable social attributes. It is not surprising that upper- and middle-class people have never been represented in the feeble-minded or educationally subnormal categories, particularly as the Wood Committee proposed to 'look to the science of Eugenics to solve the problem the sub-normal group presents to every civilised nation' (Wood Report, 1929, p. 82). Eugenic solutions comprised compulsory sterilisation and segregation.

The control aspects of social schooling have usually been

apparent in the major goals of special schooling: economic self-sufficiency and social docility. Stable feeble-minded girls were those who became domestic servants rather than prostitutes, and stable feeble-minded boys worked as labourers, and remained sober and unmarried (*Report of the Royal Commission on the Care and Control of the Feeble-Minded*, 1908; Tredgold, 1908). Post-war ESN-M schools have always been concerned to prepare their pupils for routine work, with an emphasis on punctuality and docility (Jerrold and Fox, 1968), but receiving a special education has always been a handicap in itself, particularly in times of economic recession. The connection between educational subnormality and the working class was further entrenched during the 1960s with the discovery of the new poor and 'disadvantaged'. The ideology of disadvantage was taken over as a causal explanation of non-normative categories in special education, particularly by some psychologists, and it has become a common-sense assumption that educational retardation can naturally be explained by 'environmental handicap' (Gulliford, 1969, 1971). The enormous amount of research devoted to explaining working-class failure in the education system by sociologists of education has usually subsumed the mildly subnormal under general underachievement, without noting the crucial differences and implications – social, legal, and economic – of failing to remain within the normal education system.

Those currently responsible for recommendations and legislation concerned with special education are implicitly, if not explicitly, aware that they are still largely dealing with the 'social problem' class. The Warnock Committee wrote in 1978 that:

> We are fully aware that many children with educational difficulties may suffer from familial or wider social deficiencies, while for most children their family life enhances their development, others show educational difficulties because they do not obtain from their families the quality of stimulation or sense of stability which is necessary for proper educational progress. (*Special Educational Needs* . . ., 1978, p. 4)

This is simply the old deficit argument, implying that something is lacking in child and family which was used in the creation of the 'compensatory education' ideology of the 1960s (Bernstein,

1971). However, new legislation will need to obfuscate the social selection of manual working-class and black children for the non-normative areas of special education, to prevent it being made too clear that it is still the 'social problem class' being predominantly selected for special education. It seems likely that the legislation will embody the notion in the white paper (Department of Education and Science, 1980b) that children with special needs are to include not only those whose difficulties stem from physical and mental disability, but also those 'which may be due to some other cause'. The social and behavioural deficiencies of the troublesome social problem class will thus be adequately dealt with by special education.

The rhetoric of special needs

The terminology used as a legitimation for the exclusion of more and more children from the normal education system and for placing them in a type of education which does not allow them to compete for educational credentials, and subjects them to even more social control than in normal schooling, is that of special needs. The use of the term is rapidly becoming tautological rhetoric, and its uses are more ideological than educational.

The whole concept of needs is ambiguous. The vocabulary of needs in education stems from the progressive child-centred movement (Barrow, 1978), and was originally inspired by Rousseau's discussion about true and artificial needs (Rosseau, 1762). Rousseau wrote of his mythical pupil Émile: 'give him not what he wants, but what he needs', but did not elaborate on who should decide on the need. The concept was first used officially in the discussion of special educational treatment provided by the Ministry of Education in 1946. Without modification, ordinary schools, primary and secondary, could not 'meet the needs' of the children placed in the categories of handicap (Ministry of Education, 1946). While this was a defence of categorisation, it was also a rationalisation for the removal of children from normal school.

The concept of needs, as we have noted, has been elaborated by philosophers concerned to play down the political connotations of who decides that others have 'needs'. The terminology of needs was also taken up by psychologists concerned with special education, which is perhaps not surprising, as psychologists are accustomed to think in individualistic terms. Gulliford elaborated on the notion of special education needs in his book of that title published in 1971. Parts of chapter 3 of the 1978 Warnock Report urging 'the merits of a more positive approach [to special education] based on the concept of special educational need' bear a remarkable resemblance to chapter 1 of Gulliford's (1971) book. Gulliford was concerned to explain much of supposed 'need' in terms of cultural disadvantage, and confused normative and non-normative categories as though the latter were unproblematic.

> We have moved a long way from simple ideas about a few
> major defects, blindness, deafness, physical or mental defect.
> We think rather of special educational needs, which may arise
> from personal disabilities or environmental circumstances
> and often from a combination of the two. (Gulliford, 1971,
> p. 5)

Anticipating, or assisting, the Warnock Committee, Gulliford also recommended that special needs could be met 'in special school, in special classes or units in ordinary school or be the subject of some extra attention and care within the ordinary work of schools' (Gulliford, 1971).

Part of the rhetoric of special needs includes the attempt to present whatever passes for special education as a benevolent 'good' for individual children. It involves seeing children outside a social context. Thus, during the 1960s the DES noted tautologically that: 'special education is education which is specially well adapted to meet a child's needs' (Department of Education and Science, 1965, p. 1) and Cave and Maddison, reviewing research on special education for the Warnock Committee, wrote that 'special education is, in effect no more and no less than education that is so well adapted to a child's needs that he is able to develop to his full capacity' (Cave and Maddison, 1978, p. 12). This led to the debatable claim that 'all education must become special' (Tizard, 1974). This is debatable because special education is a clearly defined legal sub-section of education, into which children can be placed without the consent of their parents (Tomlinson, 1981). Similarly, despite the benevolent rhetoric, special needs is a mystifying concept directing attention away from the needs that are actually being served by the expansion of special education. It is significant that the DES circular elaborating on 'the discovery of children requiring special education and an assessment of their needs' (Department of Education and Science, 1975a) first used the word 'need' in the context of being able to 'detect children who show deviations from the wide range of normality', and of parents' 'need' to recognise that their child requires special education. The 'needs of the children' are only mentioned on the last page of the circular in the context of transfer back to normal school. Needs in special education are by no means confined to the children. They relate more to the needs of normal education to remove children and the 'interest' of the professionals involved. Mary Wilson articulated this well in her comment that:

> the definition of special education in terms of needs rather than disabilities should remove the doubts of some administrators about the place of disadvantaged and disruptive pupils in the system. The question whether a disruptive child is or is not maladjusted will in future be of only academic interest. Some teachers may question whether a disruptive teenager is suffering from a disability of mind, but are unlikely to doubt that he has special needs. (Wilson, 1980)

It is the need of school and teacher to function unimpeded by troublesome pupils that is paramount, rather than any needs of children. The National Union of Teachers recognised this need clearly in the response to the Warnock Committee; the union hoped that the definition of 'need' would not be too broad, otherwise local education authorities might evade their responsibilities for providing special education (National Union of Teachers, 1979). The NUT, of course, represents both the interests of normal educators in removing children and the interests of special educators in gaining clients.

Much discussion of 'need' in special education has turned out to be discussion of 'provision'. The National Association of Special Education devoted its annual conference in 1966 to a discussion of 'what is special education?' After ritually noting the needs of children, the whole conference was devoted to a discussion of provision for specific handicaps (National Association for Special Education, 1966). Similarly, the Warnock Committee, after adopting the concept of special needs, in capital letters on page 37, and promising an analysis of the concept, did so in two paragraphs (3–19 and 3–40) solely in terms of provision: provision of equipment, facilities, resources, curricula, teachers, and other professionals and provision of a particular social and emotional climate.

Needs are relative, historically, socially and politically. The important point is that some groups have the power to define the needs of others, and to decide what provision shall be made for these predetermined needs. The unproblematic acceptance of 'special need' in education rests upon the acceptance that there are foolproof assessment processes which will correctly diagnose and define the needs of children. But the rhetoric of special needs may have become more of a rationalisation by which people who have power to define and shape the system of special education and who have vested interests in the assessment of, and provision of, more and more children as special, maintain their influence and interests. The rhetoric of special needs may be humanitarian, the practice is control and vested interests.

The use of the term special is also becoming problematic, particularly as this terminology has recently had specific links with forces of order and control. For example, we have the Special Patrol Group and Special Air Services. Richmond deplored the continued use of the word special, as 'an identification in pragmatic terms, which will ensure the very division between handicapped and non-handicapped which the [Warnock] committee is determined to eliminate' (Richmond, 1979). He considered that there is nothing special about schools ensuring they are teaching effectively, that children are learning, that the curriculum is appropriate, that there is a suitable environment with advice and support. This comment has overtones of the point made by Basil Bernstein concerning compensatory education in 1970, when he wrote: 'I do not understand how we can talk about offering compensatory education to children who, in the first place, have not as yet been offered an adequate educational environment' (Bernstein, 1970).

Rephrased, it is the egalitarian notion that it is distasteful to segregate out and offer a special education to children who have not actually been offered an adequate normal education that is partially responsible for the debate on integration.

Integration

After a hundred years spent building a complex sub-system of special education and segregating particular children out of normal education, there is currently a move towards the reintegration of children into what have become known in America as 'less restrictive environments'. The move in Britain has been more succinctly described by Kirp as 'opening the door to the gilded cage' (Kirp, 1980).

It is the integration debate that has forced all those concerned with special education to justify or attempt to legitimate their own views and interests. The debate has begun to allow a discussion of special education in wider social, political and educational terms than was possible when segregation was legitimated by an ideology of benevolent humanitarianism. The integration debate has led to some examination of the actual purpose and functions of special education and the question raised in chapter 1 becomes most relevant here: why, if special education developed to exclude troublesome children and thus serve the interests of the normal education system, political interests in social control and expanding professional interests, is the integration debate taking place at all?

One answer to this is that special education has always provided something of a dilemma of egalitarianism. It is not surprising that Sweden, the country best known for its egalitarian tendencies, was the first country to build up an expensive and elaborate special education system only to consider dismantling it and 'mainstreaming' or 'normalising' the children again. Werner-Putnam, in the context of examining the types of special education developed in 120 countries, has pointed out that in countries like Sweden which have reached a zenith in providing for as many handicaps as possible, the next step appears to be 'a gradual decrease in the number of students in special education' (Werner-Putnam, 1979). She argues quite reasonably that countries which have not yet provided segregated schooling would do well to provide mainstream facilities for all handicapped children and by-pass the stage of separate schooling.

But it was in the USA that egalitarian distaste for segregating children was taken most seriously. A series of congressional hearings in Washington during 1975 led to the discovery that half of the estimated eight million handicapped children in the USA were not receiving the educational services they needed or were entitled to and many children were being placed in 'inappropriate educational settings because of undetected handicap or as a violation of their individual rights' (Zettel, 1978). This last point was partly a response to pressure from the black community who were concerned at the number of black children placed in schools and classes for the educationally mentally retarded, (Cookson, 1978). As in Britain, egalitarian dilemmas in special education centred on the implicit acknowledgment that two-thirds of 'handicapped' children fall into the non-normative categories of mildly retarded, and/or maladjusted, and are mainly working-class and/ or black children.

Public Law 94–142 (The Education of Handicapped Children) Act became law in 1978 in the USA and the egalitarian philosophy behind the act is 'mainstreaming wherever possible'. Every handicapped child is to be provided with an Individualised Educational Program (IEP) and 'removal of handicapped children from the regular educational environment occurs only when the nature of severity of the handicap is such that education in regular classes with the use of supplementary aids and services cannot be achieved satisfactorily' (Zettel, 1978).

Pocklington, asking what lessons Britain can learn from American experiences of integration, was enthusiastic that PL 94–142 had, despite teething troubles and resistance, profoundly influenced special education, largely by making special education a general concern, and forcing confrontation between school systems responsible for general and special education (Pocklington, 1980).

The point reached in the integration debate in Britain by 1980 clearly indicated that egalitarian notions of integration conflicted with the political need to ensure that children could, if necessary, be removed from normal classrooms. Thus, the 1980 white paper accepted initially that:

> the government takes as its starting point the principle that children and young people who have such [special educational] needs should be educated in association with those who do not [and] intends that the planned and sensible integration of handicapped children into ordinary schools

should continue. (Department of Education and Science, 1980b, p. 13)

However,

for some children with special needs association, or full association, with other children is the wrong solution and to impose it would be unfair to the child, his parents, other children and the tax payer.

This ambivalence was certainly underpinned by the Warnock Committee who, in recommending the extension of the concept of 'special' to one in five children, added 'the great majority of children with special educational needs will have to be not only identified but also helped within the normal school'. Mary Warnock herself has written that ordinary schools must expect to cater for more children with special needs and 'the whole concept of children with peculiar difficulties (or indeed peculiar talents) must be a natural part of the comprehensive ideal' (Warnock, 1980a).

This expresses the egalitarian belief that a common school must cater for bright and dull, talented and handicapped. But what sort of integration will the comprehensive ideal produce? The Warnock Committee distinguished between three forms of integration. *Locational* – that is, special units or classes in an ordinary school or a special school on the same site as an ordinary school; *social* – where locational integration exists, but 'social interchange' also takes place between special and normal; and *functional* integration, which involves special children almost joining their normal peers in regular classes on a full- or part-time basis.

The Warnock recommendations and the government approach do go some way towards accommodating egalitarian critics of segregation, while keeping what counts as 'special need' as vague as possible in order to accommodate segregation where it is deemed necessary. Functional integration, for example, could still ensure that a disruptive child is removed from his or her normal classroom and tagged with the label of 'special', which, as chapter 2 demonstrated, carries a historical stigma of difference and inferiority.

The integration debate is also a debate about resources, provision, and the vested interests of professionals. It was not surprising that teachers in both normal and special education were initially less than enthusiastic about integration, particularly as it was first presented, in the form of section 10 of the 1976 Education Act. Normal teachers have for years had interests in the removal of troublesome children from their classrooms, special teachers have claims to skills and expertise in dealing with a variety of handicapped children and would obviously be anxious to retain a clientele in special schools or classes, or if integration became inevitable, to claim and offer expertise within the normal school situation. The National Union of Teachers' reply to the Warnock Committee used financial arguments to press the case against integration: 'The Union is very concerned that local authorities, under pressure to cut expenditure, may use integration as a means of saving money by placing handicapped children in ordinary schools without adequate support' (National Union of Teachers, 1979).

The union stressed that particular groups of pupils, particularly the severely maladjusted and those of extremely limited ability, 'may present insuperable problems for teachers in the ordinary classroom situation' (National Union of Teachers, 1979, p. 14).

The union argued that integration would involve considerable expense, a point supported by evidence from America (Pockington, 1980), particularly in terms of developing special units in ordinary schools, adapting classrooms, and training additional staff, but government argued back that falling rolls would affect special as well as normal schools and that 'this would also serve to ease the pressure on resources' (DES, 1980b, p. 9). The Warnock Committee had noted that more spending on the handicapped would ultimately save public money, by ensuring that more of the handicapped grow up self-sufficient, but by the end of 1980 Mary Warnock herself was conceding that: 'It is impossible for the government to put money in now', and was also advocating LEAs taking places in private education for pre-school special children (Warnock, 1980b, p. 8).

The debate over resources is, of course, a familiar one. It is the permanent economic dilemma of special education; how to provide as cheaply as possible for the handicapped, while at the same time ensuring that as many as possible grow up productive and self-sufficient.

Currently, some practitioners in ordinary and special education are engaged in producing organisational and curriculum solutions on an *ad hoc* basis. It is their efforts which will actually create the reality of 'provision for special needs' within integrated schools. The situation in Oxfordshire, described by Jones (1981), where 'integration' was presented as a *fait accompli* by the local authority, provides a good illustration of the variety of conflicts and problems which are emerging with the attempted dismantling of segregated provision.

It is resources and vested interests, rather than egalitarianism, which are more likely to determine the outcome of the integration debate. The anxieties of teachers in normal and special schools that integration may be forced on them have so far been allayed by research findings, which point to organisation, staffing and planning difficulties. Thus, a survey in Bradford 'allays any fears that ordinary schools will be presented with large numbers of children who exhibit emotional problems, or that special schools will become unnecessary' (*Educational Research News*, 33, 1980), and the work of Hegarty *et al.* has pointed to the effects of makeshift arrangements and inefficient planning for integration (Hegarty, 1980; Hegarty *et al.*, 1981).

The idea of integration has become partly confused by the conflation of normative and non-normative categories of handicap or need. Crudely, teachers in normal schools may be willing to accommodate the 'ideal' child with special needs in their classrooms – the bright, brave child in a wheelchair – they will still want to be rid of the actual 'average' child with special needs – the dull disruptive child.

The integration debate leads back to the purpose of categorisation, discussed at the beginning of this chapter. The state education system developed over the past hundred years with a 'safety-valve' – that of the exclusion of certain children, particularly those from the 'social problem class', into a separate sub-system. This was originally legitimated by careful categorisation, but now will be legitimated by the rhetoric of 'special needs', even if exclusion only amounts to the room next door!

The dilemmas discussed in this chapter lead to a conclusion that special education will continue, in different forms, as a permanent sub-system of the education system. It may appear to be, in Werner-Putnam's words, ready to be 'dismantled' (1979), but it is the terminology, forms, and ideologies that are changing, the underlying functions and purposes remain.

The book now moves on to discuss the most important quesions current in special education. Who decides on the 'special education needs' of children and how do they accomplish this? How do professionals assess children?

Chapter Four · Professional roles and the assessment process

The most crucial aspect of special education is the assessment process. This is literally the point at which certain children are judged to be different from others – to have 'special needs' which necessitate their removal from the normal educational process offered to the majority of children in schools. The claim that the special needs of children are being met rests on the assumption that there is some sort of foolproof assessment mechanism by which children with special needs can be identified. But this is highly problematic. As the twentieth century has progressed, faith in the objectivity and scientific validity of mental testing has diminished (Kamin, 1977; Broadfoot, 1979) and the power of professional experts to judge and decide what is best for others has come under more scrutiny (Johnson, 1972; Jackson, 1970). Historically, the crucial professions involved in ascertaining, as the 1944 Act put it, children for special education have been medical, psychological and educational (both pedagogic and administrative), and, as chapter 2 has demonstrated, there have always been some antipathy and power struggles between these professionals. Over the past twenty years more professionals have come to claim expertise in dealing with children moving into, or in, special education; child psychiatrists, social workers, assessment centre staff, remedial teachers, education welfare officers, probation and careers officers, community health workers, counsellors, speech therapists, and behavioural therapists are some of the groups who claim a right to involvement in special education.

It is the professional status of these people – particularly those of the older established professions – their judgments, and the power implicit in these judgments, which legitimates the complex assessment procedures which have developed for assessing children thought to be in need of special education. This chapter discusses some of the characteristics and powers of professional people as they relate to special education, documents the offical procedures and professional involvement which have developed since 1944, then, using examples from a study of professional involvement in ascertaining children from ESN-M education, illustrates the way in which professionals actually work in the assessment process.

Characteristics and powers of professionals

The development of special education has been marked by a vast increase in the number of professionals who serve a clientele which they have vested interests in expanding. Literally, the more children thought to be in need of special education the more work for the professionals. Why is it then, that professional judgments are sought and accepted?

Professionals claim 'expert' knowledge and they profess to know better than others what is wrong with their clients or their clients' affairs. The esoteric knowledge of professionals, as Everett Hughes has pointed out, often cannot be explained to the client and its base is not always clear (Hughes, 1965). Armed with their expert knowledge, professionals ask to be trusted; they do not expect their clients to question their judgments, and even though they are employed in areas of universal social concern, they have to persuade people that their expertise and advice is more valuable than the advice of interested, caring lay people. They not only claim to know better, they do not expect their clients to be true judges of the value of the services they receive (Hughes, 1965). A further key professional characteristic is the 'service ideal'; professionals profess to serve the community with a detachment and an absence of personal interest which might influence their actions and advice.

Much of this contributes to what Halsey has called 'group charisma' (Halsey, 1970) or what Larson has called the professional mystique (Larson, 1977). She points out that a major professional characteristic is in fact that professionals are members of socially dominant groups. 'The relative superiority over, and distance from the working class, is one of the major characteristics that all professions, and would-be professions have in common'

(Larson, 1977, p. xvi). Professionals are outside and above the working-class clientele who accept the 'mystique' that professionals do possess superior ability and rational knowledge. Indeed, professional powers and privileges depend upon this professional ability to create an aura of mystery around their work while at the same time selling their labour and conforming to bureaucratic practices.

In the last century professionals could be described as liberal capitalists, they were not servants of the state. But nowadays doctors are largely employed by the state via the health service and psychologists and teachers are employed by the state via local education authorities. Despite this, it is in the interests of professionals to preserve their (essentially upper-middle- and middle-class) privileges – salaries and status – by enlarging their clientele and creating a mystique about their work.

But the service of professionals is essential to the state, particularly in terms of legitimating the treatment of certain groups of potentially troublesome people, such as the clients of special education. Larson asserts that professional judgments exert a form of ideological control over people, the expertise sometimes being used to validate what are, in effect, measures of social control. For example, without the mystique of professional judgments it is doubtful whether many parents would accept that their children had 'special needs' which meant that they were excluded from full normal education. The professional mystique may be particularly relevant in special education, as this is an area where many clients do not come voluntarily. The techniques of professional persuasion usually work in encouraging reluctant parents to allow their children to be placed in special education, but enforceable procedures are built into the law. These enforceable procedures[1] have always made it difficult for professionals to claim that their assessment decisions are purely objective and motivated by humanitarian concern. They seldom mention to parents that coercion can be used if persuasion fails. Likewise, one of the most powerful aids to professional people is the secret nature of the assessment processes. Despite moves during the 1970s to open up areas where confidential files were the rule, future legislation is envisaged which will still incorporate a secret aspect. The 1980 white paper recommended that procedures for children who are to be 'recorded' as in need of special education should remain secretive: 'It would be wrong to require full disclosure to parents of the professional reports behind the recording. Professional reports must remain confidential if they are to give the LEA. . . the information it needs in meeting special educational needs' (Department of Education and Science, 1980b, p. 18). Professional mystique is complemented by secrecy; parents and children in special education assessment have little choice but to trust the professionals. This is particularly true with medical professional involvement in special education, since the confidential nature of medical records and the trust demanded by medical practitioners spills over into the whole of special education. For a minority of the children designated as handicapped since 1945, medical expertise alone has 'diagnosed' and 'treated' and arguments over whether medical science is increasing or decreasing the number of handicapped children have taken place. For example, claims that medical science 'keeps alive' more children with serious defects and disabilities have been matched by claims that genetic counselling has reduced the incidence of handicap. Nevertheless, the involvement of medicine, the archetypal profession, with its social image of service and devotion to human welfare, has meant that an extra demand for trust and deference to mystique are carried over and expected from parents whose children are potentially in need of special education.

Professionals are thus very powerful people in the assessment processes. But sociologists have become increasingly interested in the way in which state bureaucracies have harnessed the expertise of professionals to legitimate the way in which subordinate groups in a society can be controlled, even though ultimately legal sanctions might be available for the state to use. The legitimation which professional judgments give in special education does ultimately depend on coercion by law, but a majority of the clients in special education will be persuaded by 'expertise', rather than coerced by law. It should also be stressed again that the majority of parents with children in special education are of a lower social class than the professionals who deal with them, and persuasion becomes a powerful tool when based on the acceptance of, or acquiescence in, professional superiority and mystique.

Professionals and the official assessment procedures

The official procedures developed to move children into special education are very complex, and an ideology has developed that a process of 'smooth teamwork' operates between all the professionals, which allows for the 'needs' of the child to be assessed. Any notion of conflict in the processes has always been played down and the development of extended multi-professional assessment certainly assumes an unrealistic degree of co-operation, communication and absence of professional jealousies and anxieties. The notion of a 'team' decision dates back to the first selection procedures for schools for special instruction in the 1890s, when medical and educational personnel attempted to control the selection procedures and the science of psychology was not yet developed. By 1944 the 'team' was composed of medical, educational and psychological personnel, and the development of mental testing had enhanced psychological influence in the procedures. Educational pedagogical influence on assessment procedures had declined by then, but educational-administrative involvement was much more apparent. Medical officers were the only professionals to have statutory powers to decide that a child was suffering from 'a disability of body or mind' (1944 Education Act).

The extent of increasing professional involvement in assessment for special education from 1945 to the present is illustrated by Figures 4.1, 4.2 and 4.3.

Professional expertise, during this time, was officially directed towards demonstrating that a child had a 'disability of body or mind' and needed special educational treatment. Professional decisions and judgments were recorded on the Handicapped Pupils forms 1–5, form 3 HP being filled out by the head teacher of a school referring a child, 2 HP being completed by a doctor and psychologist, and, in the event of parental objection, 1 HP being filled out by a senior medical officer. This called on the medical officer to certify the category of handicap into which a child fell. Medical officers were even empowered, providing they had done a short course on the administration of psychological tests, to test children and fill in the psychological section of the form. In practice, although requirements varied between local education authorities, psychologists often wrote lengthy reports

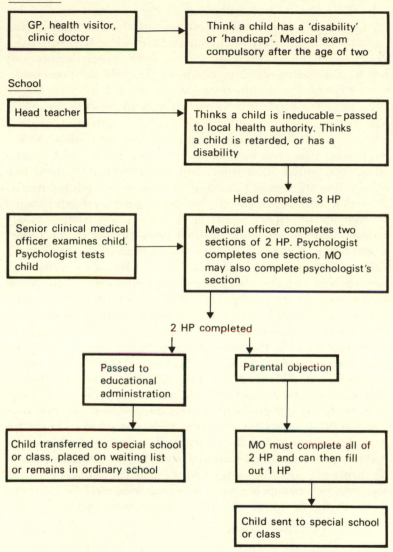

Pre-school

| GP, health visitor, clinic doctor | → | Think a child has a 'disability' or 'handicap'. Medical exam compulsory after the age of two |

School

| Head teacher | → | Thinks a child is ineducable – passed to local health authority. Thinks a child is retarded, or has a disability |

Head completes 3 HP

| Senior clinical medical officer examines child. Psychologist tests child | → | Medical officer completes two sections of 2 HP. Psychologist completes one section. MO may also complete psychologist's section |

2 HP completed

Passed to educational administration

Parental objection

Child transferred to special school or class, placed on waiting list or remains in ordinary school

MO must complete all of 2 HP and can then fill out 1 HP

Child sent to special school or class

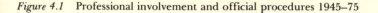

Figure 4.1   Professional involvement and official procedures 1945–75

on children they had seen in addition to providing an IQ score.

By 1976 the recommendations of the government Circular 2/75 on the discovery and assessment of children with special educational needs, were being put into operation; HP forms were discontinued to be replaced with new SE (special education) forms, and professional involvement and official procedures from 1975 became as illustrated in Figure. 4.2.

Form SE1 was to be the 'report by a Head Teacher on a child who may require special education', SE2 was to be a 'medical report on a child who may require special education', SE3 a 'report by a psychologist on a child who may require special education', and SE4 a summary and action sheet on the needs of a child requiring special education. It was suggested in Circular 2/75 that SE4 be filled out by an experienced educational psychologist or adviser in special education, which immediately raised problems as to whether the major influence on this report would be psychological or educational-administrative. SE5 was a new version of the old 'certification' form, 1 HP – to be completed by a medical officer if the parents of a child objected to special education. The procedures after 1975 still left the only statutory powers in medical hands, and psychologists, in particular, felt that this was unfair to them. In a study in one LEA in 1976, a psychologist said 'at the smell of a medical decision, we will all be back working under the old medical terms' (Tomlinson, 1981).

The decentralisation of the English education system means that local education authorities do have considerable autonomy to interpret central government recommendations in their own way, and this allows for differing local procedures. The 1976 study found that in one large city the chief administrative office had formerly been an educational psychologist, which meant that the profession of psychology had a particular influence on the way in which new procedures were implemented. The official notes for the professional staff in the city read that

> Referral may be made by schools, other agencies or parents, but the normal practice in B. will be that children apparently in need of special education because of learning or behaviour difficulties will be referred to a psychologist in the first instance, whereas children with actual or suspected physical or sensory handicap will first be referred by a medical officer. (Tomlinson, 1981)

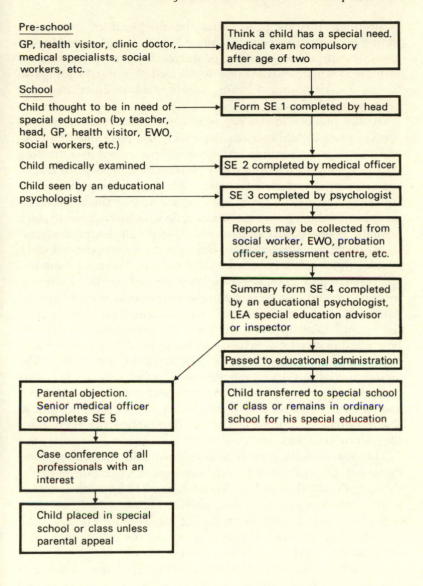

Pre-school

GP, health visitor, clinic doctor, medical specialists, social workers, etc. ⟶ Think a child has a special need. Medical exam compulsory after age of two

School

Child thought to be in need of special education (by teacher, head, GP, health visitor, EWO, social workers, etc.) ⟶ Form SE 1 completed by head

Child medically examined ⟶ SE 2 completed by medical officer

Child seen by an educational psychologist ⟶ SE 3 completed by psychologist

Reports may be collected from social worker, EWO, probation officer, assessment centre, etc.

Summary form SE 4 completed by an educational psychologist, LEA special education advisor or inspector

Passed to educational administration

Parental objection. Senior medical officer completes SE 5

Child transferred to special school or class or remains in ordinary school for his special education

Case conference of all professionals with an interest

Child placed in special school or class unless parental appeal

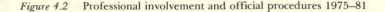

Figure 4.2   Professional involvement and official procedures 1975–81

Although this suggested that the workload of assessment should be neatly shared into assumed medical and psychological areas of competence, neither profession was completely happy with the arrangements. As one doctor said, 'I ignore headings on forms, I write what I want, I write about emotional and behavioural difficulties.'

Official practice in this city was that after assessment 'special services place a child in accordance with SE4 recommendations', and a clerk in the administration would be involved in contacting special schools and arranging a placement, unless professional disagreement necessitated a case conference. Some professionals considered that this procedure was secretive as the administration was not obliged to reveal the criteria which were used to place a child. As one psychologist noted: 'We do all this professional work, make careful decisions, then some sixteen-year-old clerk decides which school to send a child to.' The Warnock Committee, reporting in 1978, suggested new procedures by which professionals could discover and assess children in need of special education, and the 1980 white paper indicated that new legislation would take up some of these recommendations. Official policy and professional involvement as indicated by the Warnock Report and the white paper is illustrated by Figure 4.3. The recommendations and suggested new policies would certainly extend professional involvement and cater for the interests of a wide variety of professional people. As Everett Hughes put it, 'Professionals do not merely serve, they define the very wants they serve' (Hughes, 1971).

The Warnock Report recommended, and the white paper endorsed, the multi-professional examination of children under the age of two – the age laid down by the 1944 Education Act for medical examination of young children if these children were thought to have severe and complex disabilities. Otherwise, the school-based assessment procedures for the vastly increased clientele intended for special education would initially depend very much on educational-pedagogic personnel, both heads and teachers in normal education, who, together with special school teachers and local authority advisors, would be working in a 'new' role as educational consultants.

New legislation envisages that the increased clientele for special education will be children notified to the LEA as having special needs, but they will not necessarily be 'recorded' children on whom a statement is maintained. Recorded children are envisaged to be the existing 2 per cent of children currently classified into one of the ten categories of handicap. The non-recorded children, presumably the 18 per cent of children who will go to make up the Warnock Report's suggestion that 20 per cent of children may have 'special needs', will largely be the children with learning difficulties, and disruptive children, whose 'needs' may very well be met in classes or units in normal schools.

Two important points which can be made about increased educational-pedagogic involvement and powers in deciding which children do have special educational needs concern the professional characteristics of teachers, and the 'needs' of teachers in normal schools. While the professional characteristics discussed at the beginning of this chapter apply relatively unambiguously to medical and psychological personnel, the professional characteristics of teachers have always been more problematic. Goode has argued (1957) that teachers tend to be regarded more as an occupational group than as professionals; C. Wright Mills referred to teachers as 'the economic proletariat of the professionals' (1951) and Etzioni placed teachers among the 'semi-professionals' (Etzioni, 1969).

Within the occupational group of teachers special school teachers have historically been regarded as a lower-status subgroup. This was nicely illustrated by a comment from a special school head-teacher who wrote that:

> special school teachers were felt to have left the main field of education and were looked on as missionaries going into an unknown field . . . teachers in ordinary schools were glad that some of their profession had elected to do what they felt was distasteful . . . cope with defective children. (Lindsey, 1957)

Teachers are not always regarded by clients – parents and pupils – as having expert, superior knowledge; they are not always trusted implicitly; they do not have the mystique of other professions; and they will undoubtedly face more problems of legitimation in persuading parents that their children have special needs, particularly if those needs are to be catered for in ordinary schools. On the other hand, increased pedagogic involvement will undoubtedly raise the status and power of special school teachers, if their 'special' expertise is to be used as a tool to help persuade parents and to enlarge a 'special' clientele.

On the second point, that of whose 'needs' the new procedures for non-recorded children will cater for, a review of the historical development of special education has indicated that the very pupils which teachers in normal schools found most problematic in terms of the obstruction of the goals of normal education were pupils who had learning or behaviour difficulties, that is, pupils who cannot or do not want to conform to a 'normal' classroom. Teachers in normal classrooms undoubtedly have vested interests in continuing to define these kinds of troublesome children as having 'special needs' and making sure they are removed from the normal classroom. Similarly, for the first time in the history of professional special school teaching since the 1890s there is an opportunity for 'special' teachers to have real involvement in the selection and expansion of their clientele, a satisfaction of their needs if not of their clients'.

The extended multi-professional assessment for children who are to be 'recorded' if they progress beyond stage 3 of new assessment procedures can be followed in Figure 4.3. The Warnock Committee suggested that after a head teacher, medical officer and psychologist, with other possible ancillary professionals, had referred and assessed a child and recorded their views on an SE form, a form might also be provided for parents to fill in for the social services department. However, the 1980 white paper did not take this suggestion up, nor did the government take up the suggestion of a named person, to be appointed to hurry along what has always been a lengthy process. The Warnock Committee envisaged that a child might need extended multi-professional assessment, particularly at stage 5 of the proceedings and that 'other specialists' may be involved 'from narrower specialisms or perhaps with geographically wider responsibilities' (*Special Educational Needs* . . ., 1978, p. 62). These specialists would be primarily medically oriented and it was at this point in the suggested new educational procedures instigated by an LEA that the Warnock Committee had to recognise possible conflicts with medically instigated assessment of handicap procedures.

The *Report of the Committee on Child Health Services in* 1976 (Court Report) had recommended the establishment of district handicap teams to investigate and care for handicapped children,

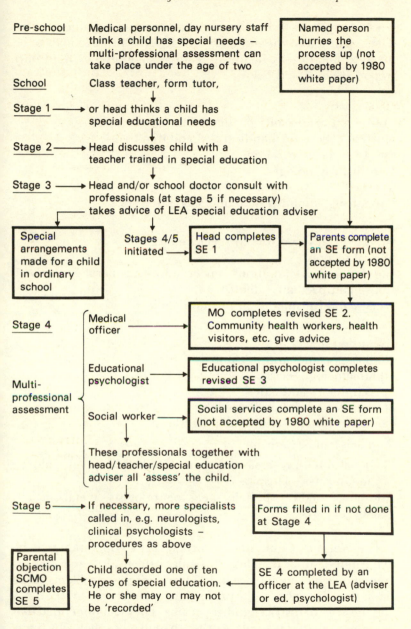

Figure 4.3 Professional involvement and the official policy as suggested by the Warnock Report and the 1980 white paper

particularly those to be discovered and assessed at an early age. The expansion in the numbers and types of professionals to be involved in a district handicap team as suggested by the Court Report is illustrated below.

Basic staff:
Consultant community paediatrician
Nursing officer for handicapped children
Specialist social workers
Principal psychologist
Teacher
Supporting administration and secretarial staff

Links with:
Advisors and inspectors in special education
Special schools
Independent organisations concerned with general education
Consultant paediatric dentist
Nurses and consultants in mental handicap
Parents

Expansion of:
Audiology clinics and personnel
Ophthalmology service
Speech theory and aides
Services for adult handicapped
Child psychiatrists and mental handicap

Regional handicap team

'Regional multi-professional centres for handicapped children
. . . in University Hospitals'
Additional medical specialists, e.g. neurologists, 'metabolic and genetic' experts

The Warnock Committee recorded that co-operation may be made more, rather than less, difficult by the health services reorganisation which took place in 1974, and foresaw problems in the similarities between multi-professional assessment by the LEA and the work of district handicap teams. They recommended that assessment should take place other than in a hospital, which was not a suggestion likely to be favoured by doctors. An article on 'School Doctors and Warnock' in 1978 noted that:

unless there is complete co-operation between those setting up a district handicap team and those organising the multi-professional assessment team, the whole process may become excessively drawn out and the fact that certain professionals may be members of both teams would not necessarily prevent bureaucratic delay. (Cash, 1978)

An illustration of the difficulties of multi-professional assessment was provided by the 1976 study in which one child was discovered to have been passed around to five doctors during her assessment process, in addition to being seen by psychologists, educational- ists and social workers. A senior clinical medical officer explained the case thus:

Dr J. [school MO] referred Mary to her own GP, who referred her to Dr O. [consultant paediatrician] who then passed her back to me. I told Dr J. to refer the girl to Dr B. [psychiatrist], but Dr B. said she wasn't going back to that school [that the girl attended]. (Tomlinson, 1981)

It was not surprising that this girl's parents were thoroughly bewildered and antagonistic to the whole assessment procedure, despite official recommendations which during the 1970s have stressed the need for parental involvement and co-operation.

What are the implications of this plethora of increased profes- sional involvement in assessment for special education? First, the interests of all professionals and semi-professionals will be catered for in that they will all have more clients and more work; the expertise and areas of competence of all professionals will be expanded, particularly those in the educational-pedagogic and medical spheres. Second, the power of increased professional expertise will increasingly be felt by the clients of special educa- tion – parents and children, who will have more experts to per- suade or coerce them into accepting that their children have special needs. Third, the professional conflicts of interests and anxiety over status and areas of competence being encroached upon are likely to undermine the ideology of 'smooth teamwork'. Official descriptions of consensus and harmony in deciding on children's special needs and how to cater for them may become less realistic and harder to defend.

The next section provides an illustration of the way in which professionals actually worked together in the ascertainment of children for one type of special education, ESN-M, demonstrating the difficulties inherent in recognising an administrative category (let alone a 'need') and the conflicts endemic in the process.

Professionals and ESN-M assessment

The ESN-M category, as we have noted in chapter 3, can be described as a non-normative category. That is, despite a variety of official descriptions of this administrative category of handicap given since 1945, there is no agreement as to what actually constitutes an ESN-M child and what, between 1945 and 1981, separated an ESN-M child from a remedial or slow-learning child. In the study undertaken in the mid-1970s (reported in Tomlinson, 1981) all professionals who had made a decision on a group of forty children passing through the referral and assessment processes for ESN-M school, were interviewed. This involved some 80 professionals – referring head teachers, special school head teachers, medical officers, psychologists and others. At the outset of the research a series of ten possible 'accounts' of ESN-M children were abstracted from the literature on subnormality, government acts, curricula, etc., and initial interviews. These accounts are recorded in Table 4.1.

It was envisaged that the professionals who referred and assessed the children would give different accounts of 'what is' an ESN-M child and thus demonstrate the problematic nature of professional assessment. It was also envisaged that conflicts due to poor professional communication and professional anxieties and jealousies might make the notion of smooth teamwork problematic.

Head teachers

Head teachers of ordinary schools are a crucial element in the ascertainment processes for special education, particularly for the non-normative categories. It is their judgment that a child is potentially ESN-M that sets in train the whole procedure. Heads overwhelmingly use functional and behavioural criteria in accounting for ESN-M children, they are not particularly

TABLE 4.1 Accounts of Educational Subnormality

1	Functional	1	Child cannot do X (X may be social, educational technological, but is usually connected to attainment, 'learning' or intellectual functioning)
		2	Child cannot communicate adequately
2	Statistical	1	Child has a 'low' IQ as measured on standardised tests
		2	Child falls into lowest 1% (or 20%) of school population in school achievement
3	Behavioural	1	Child is disruptive, troublesome, uncontrolled
		2	Child exhibits bizarre, odd, non-conformist behaviour
		3	Child unable to behave 'appropriately'
4	Organic		Child has:
		1	Genetic disorder or 'innate incapacity'
		2	Pre-natal or birth 'damage'
		3	Organic or metabolic disorder
		4	Medically demonstrable 'illness' or 'condition'
5	Psychological	1	Child is 'emotionally disturbed'
6	Social		Child has:
		1	Family with low socio-economic status; father semi- or unskilled
		2	Family 'disorganised' – poor maternal care, single parent, working mother, etc.
		3	Poor or different socialisation techniques
		4	Adverse material factors – poor housing, bad physical environment
		5	Cultural deficiency – poor cultural milieux; poor preparation for school
7	School	1	Unsatisfactory school conditions
		2	Normal school rejects child
		3	Child rejects school, i.e. truants
8	Statutory	1	Child may be 'certified' as in need of special education
9	Intuitive	1	Child has 'something wrong with him'
10	Tautological	1	Child is in need of special educational treatment

interested in causal explanations – they are interested in action. The head teachers interviewed in the research used intuitive judgments to decide who was potentially ESN-M, and felt they could distinguish between a backward 'remedial' and an ESN-M child, although there was no consensus on whether backward children were usually also disruptive or not, in the normal school. The study indicates that head teachers felt some antipathy towards educational psychologists – there was disagreement over the 'accounts' offered by these two groups of professionals – psychologists seldom used behavioural accounts of ESN-M children, whereas it was important to heads that children who were disruptive in their schools, were removed. Heads felt that while psychologists did possess special skills for assessing, particularly testing skills, they were too slow, too busy, or a very scarce resource. A few heads felt that psychologists' skills amounted to a mystique of 'IQ and long words' which could baffle and frustrate the referring school.

Heads showed less antipathy towards the medical officers whose duty it was to examine children put forward for special education – partly because they have little contact with the MOs and considered them to be less important than the psychologists in the decision-making process. They were often unaware that long delays for medical examination could hold up the assessment process and tended to blame the psychologists and the administration for delays. A few heads had realised that they could 'play off' psychological and medical personnel, by re-referring children if they did not get satisfaction. One head had referred a child whom he was anxious to have removed from the school – the psychologist was adamant that the child was 'not ESN-M' and would not recommend special schooling. The head had quietly re-referred the child to the medical officer who was more sympathetic. Heads of normal schools did not have much contact with ESN-M schools and they tended to have idealised views about the schools. One head said: 'they have better staffing ratios and the staff have all done a special one-year course' – of a school where only one member of staff had any 'special' qualifications. Heads of normal schools tended to regard ESN-M schools as places where children with learning and behavioural difficulties should go as soon as possible.

Heads thought that parents 'ought' to be involved and consulted over the referral process and by and large fulfilled their responsibility to discuss the referral with the parents. However, they did not fully understand the importance placed on discussion by parents (as we shall see in the next chapter). They were really more concerned to persuade parents not to object to special education than to offer information — as one head put it — 'no matter how we try to present is, it's still the barmy school we are sending their kids to'.

The changeover to the new SE forms was being implemented at the time of this study, but not all heads were familiar with the new forms. One head was annoyed at a peremptory letter he had had from a psychologist telling him to fill in new forms.

In common with the other professionals interviewed, head teachers relied on an informal network of communication to 'get things done'. In addition to official forms, they particularly relied on the telephone. One head, who felt himself to be in conflict with an incompetent administration, said that if he was sent the wrong forms to fill in, he tore them up in front of the telephone receiver! This head may have been expressing a feeling that as a means of communication no forms were adequate. Heads complained of long delays after referring children and filling in forms before they were contacted by other professionals or the administration. They generally felt that after the referral had been made events had gone beyond their control and they were relatively powerless to do anything but wait for the next profession to move in the assessment process.

Educational psychologists

Psychological involvement in assessment for special education dates from the rise of the mental testing movement, which was itself initially bound up with the selection of children for special schools. Cyril Burt, the first educational psychologist to be appointed by the London County Council in 1913, whose influence on mental testing for subnormality has already been noted, devoted three days of his working week to the development of mental tests, two days to selecting children for special schools (Hearnshaw, 1979). Psychologists are crucial figures in the process by which children move from normal to special ESN-M education. They work within a 'scientific' model of mental testing, possess certain professional skills which schools do not possess and they may or may not legitimate the head teacher's judgment that a child is ESN-M. There is a strong potentiality for conflict between heads and psychologists since, while heads traditionally use behavioural criteria to account for ESN-M children, psychologists do not. As one educational psychologist put it, 'there are still some schools where, if a kid is trouble, he's out so fast his feet don't touch the floor'. Psychologists tend to account for ESN-M children in functional and statistical terms; an ESN-M child has low attainment and he has a low IQ. They also used school accounts – an ESN-M child may be one whom his normal school has rejected – and they are able to act upon a belief that a school should cope with a child by not recommending ESN-M schooling or by not visiting the school.

Educational psychologists have no statutory role in the assessment processes and the personality and beliefs of individuals do affect the way they work. As a profession, they have considerable freedom to make idiosyncratic decisions, and their professional autonomy means that they are not necessarily accountable to others for these decisions. For example, although psychologists include IQ testing as one of their skills, one psychologist remarked that he had 'given up testing West Indian children as the tests aren't valid'. This permitted professional idiosyncrasy makes decisions difficult to question, and parents have to take the decisions on trust.

Conflicts with fellow professionals and with parents can, however, affect decisions. The only middle-class family in the study were adamant that their child should remain at normal school, even though his IQ had been given as 67, and this case provided an illustration of the way in which professional behaviour does vary with social class. By and large, educational psychologists expressed satisfaction that by the mid-1970s they had achieved parity of esteem with the medical profession in the assessment processes, but they were still wary of medical encroachment into what they regarded as their province. As one psychologist said: 'The MOs are important in the initial screening of physical attributes, but they are amazingly irrelevant in that they duplicate information, particularly if they do IQ tests and don't pass the information on to us.' Psychologists directed strong criticism at the local education authority's administration. They felt that assessment decisions should be 'a mutual balance between medical and psychological people' and that there was a danger that a 'faceless administration' would overrule their professional expertise.

Psychologists generally felt that communication between professionals would be improved with the new SE forms – they strongly disapproved of the old HP forms – but a major source of anxiety was that the new summary form SE4 might be completed by an administrator who had not actually seen the child to make a professional judgment.

The professional involvement of educational psychologists in assessment for this particular type of special education, ESN-M, indicated that by the mid-1970s, psychologists had greatly increased their powers in their (historical) struggle with the medical profession and regarded doctors as colleagues in the decision-making processes; a view not entirely shared by the medical officers.

Medical officers

The medical profession was legally to play the primary role in the ascertainment procedures for special education from 1913, and a medical examination to determine whether a child was suffering from a 'disability of mind or body' continued to be statutory after 1944. After the 1948 National Health Act the School Health Services remained under the aegis of the local education authority – principal school medical officers being responsible to the chief education officer. With the reorganisation of the Health Services in 1974 the principal school medical officer became known as the senior specialist in community medicine (child health) and it was senior clinical and clinical medical officers who had responsibility for ascertaining children in need of special education. Health service reorganisation certainly created some confusion concerning the professional tasks and responsibilities of the doctors; the overlap between multi-professional assessment at Warnock Stage 5, and the work of the district handicap teams set up after the Court Report, have already been noted. Administration of different educational and medical geographical units has also provided some problems. For example, the old pattern of school clinics in cities does not necessarily correspond to post-1974 District Health Authorities. In some respects it would seem that the educational and medical aspects of the assessment processes are becoming more, rather than less, difficult to reconcile.

In the 1976 study the doctors interviewed tended to use social accounts of ESN-M children more than any other professionals. They did not think that ESN-M children suffered from any particular medical pathology, apart from occasionally regarding the administrative category ESN-M as a handicap comparable to organic handicap. They considered the children likely to be of low social class, or 'rough children', as one doctor put it. These accounts may be tautological; as almost all children referred as potentially ESN-M are children of low socio-economic status the doctors will only be called upon to examine such children as potentially ESN-M.

The doctors' views of their role in the assessment process were somewhat contradictory. They considered their role to be mainly 'physical', but at the same time regarded it as their duty to involve themselves with the family and background of the children. 'We need to look at the whole child in his environment', as one doctor put it, but this did not appear to necessitate doctors' doing more than having parents attend their children's medical examinations.

Doctors were perhaps less willing to accept the incursion of other professionals, particularly psychologists, into what they traditionally considered to be their area of competence, and they were less willing to see themselves as part of a team. One doctor particularly, who in the 1950s had been one of two MOs responsible for assessment in the cities, said 'I felt the psychologists were taking over from us – they seldom followed up children as we did . . . I felt someone had to make the final decision and it was the doctor who was unbiased and could make a fair decision at a medical clinic.'

By and large, the doctors were happy to make educational decisions, only one young doctor thought that 'people who were not concerned with education' should not do this, and although qualified by a short course to administer tests, said that she 'seldom used her limited knowledge of tests'.

Doctors employed in the school child health services tend to be female, as one doctor put it: 'There is no career structure so what man wants to come into this branch?' It is interesting to speculate whether more conflict between the professionals would be generated if the doctors in the assessment processes were male.

In the study some conflict was apparent, between MOs and

psychologists and MOs and the administration in particular. The doctors felt embroiled in administrative and communication problems – they thought they were not always kept fully informed of decisions taken by other professionals about children, or that the administration might manipulate their decisions. They showed little enthusiasm for their SE2 form, felt that forms arrived incomplete or not at all, for their records, and 'only the telephone keeps our heads above water'.

Special school head teachers

Heads of special schools, although not directly involved in the assessment processes for special schools, do have powers to refuse a child entry, or hold up entry, to their schools. They can thus literally shape the popular notion of the 'special school child', given that a special school child is one who has attended a special school or class. In the study one head disliked taking 'violent' children into her suburban ESN-M school, and her school had a reputation for being a quiet, unobtrusive place. In another school, an integrated ESN-M and -S school, where the head prided himself on his dealing with difficult children, the local image of an ESN child was that of a 'crazy disturbed child'. The major role of special school heads in the assessment process is to collect together all the documents and forms on which other professionals had recorded their assessment decisions. But they were not too happy about the efficiency of the administration, and noted that forms were often not sent and records ended up incomplete. They did not consider that the new SE forms recorded information on children adequately, and were sometimes hostile to what they saw as an over-bureaucratic educational administration. As one head remarked: 'they are more concerned with running an efficient bureaucracy than with the needs of children'.

Heads of special ESN-M schools were somewhat ambivalent in their attitudes to psychologists – a 'useless bunch with middle-class solutions', as one head remarked, but they did regard psychologists as being more objective in their testing of children and suggestions for educational programmes in school. The 'IQ' supplied by psychologists was regarded as a valuable piece of information. They were less ambivalent in their attitudes to doctors, regarding them as people who provided a valuable service, both during the assessment process and after placement in school. They also felt that contact with referring schools was vital, attaching more importance to this than referring heads did reciprocally and they deplored their lack of contacts with normal schools. At the time of this study, 'integration' was a favourite topic of conversation, and special school heads were beginning to worry about the possible changes in the functions and clientele, and indeed about the continued existence, of their schools.

Special ESN-M school heads were as unclear about accounting for the presence of their pupils as were other professionals. They seemed to have an ideal-typical ESN-M child in mind, a dull conforming child, falling within certain IQ limits, but did not think that the majority of children in their school corresponded to this ideal. They did think that their schools were valuable places for children with a variety of problems and 'needs'. The study of professionals involved in assessment for ESN-M education demonstrated that there were differences in the way in which different professions judged children to be ESN-M. Definitions of this non-normative category allowed for judgments being based as much on the beliefs of the professionals about other social groups as on any objective criteria. If this is the case with a statutory category it could be that the criteria for defining 'special needs' could be even more problematic. In addition, the study demonstrated that although there was much co-operation between professionals and some praise for each other's professional skills, there were also conflicts over communication, anxieties over status and annoyance over perceived inadequacies. The notion of 'smooth teamwork' may be more of an ideology than a reality.

The increasing power of professionals

The adoption of the concept of special educational needs as a rationale for the separation of children in normal and special education and the abolition of statutory categories of handicap are likely to give more, rather than less, power to professionals. The new processes of referral and assessment for an expanded special sub-system will increase the number and type of professionals whose judgments will be used in the assessment process. While the assessment procedures beyond stage 3 will increase the number of psychological and medical personnel plus ancillary professionals such as social workers, educational welfare officers and so on, it is educationalists, particularly heads and teachers in normal education, who will have increased powers to decide that larger numbers of children have special needs, and it is special educators who will have expanded professional interests in making provision for these children, in special units, classes, or schools.

Professionals are increasingly being used as 'experts with rational knowledge' by state bureaucracies to solve what has been described in other contexts as a 'crisis of legitimacy' (Habermas, 1973). A crisis comes about when a system, in this case an education system, cannot rationally or politically meet the ideological commitments needed to maintain legitimacy.

There is a conflict between the egalitarian ideology of integrating all children in a common school, and the need to separate out all children who may be troublesome in the widest possible sense. The decision has already been taken to define these children on the basis of special needs, and the problems of assessing a special need are, as we have already noted, quite problematic. It is likely that the increased use of professional expertise will be used to legitimate the assessment processes that define 'special need', and professionals will become more powerful in the assessment processes. This use of professional expertise to individualise what are, in effect, social problems, provides a good illustration of what C. Wright Mills was referring to when he talked about public issues being presented as private troubles. How, then, do these processes affect the clients of special education, parents and children, and what are the experiences of both teachers and pupils in special education? These questions are taken up in the next chapter.

Chapter Five · Parents, pupils and teachers in special education

The involvement of parents in the assessment processes for special education, and in the actual education of their children in special schools and classes, is an area in which benevolent rhetoric supersedes reality. While government publications and professional groups urge the involvement of parents as equals, the available evidence indicates that many parents feel uninvolved and inadequately consulted in the assessment processes and uninformed, misinformed or overwhelmed by professional expertise when their children are actually placed in special education.

The views of children placed in special education and their experiences during assessment and in special schooling are almost totally unrecorded. The rhetoric that children's special needs are being catered for stops short of any actual enquiry into what in other contexts might be called client satisfaction. It would, of course, be accurate to point out that the process of education as experienced by children in ordinary schools is relatively unrecorded and it is only recently that studies have begun to record school form the pupils' point of view (Willis, 1977; Woods, 1980a). The fact that children in special education have already been judged 'not normal' makes it even less likely that their views or experiences would be thought to be worth recording. The clients of special education – children and their parents – have less power and are subject to more strategies of persuasion and coercion and are less likely to have their views and opinions recorded than in any other part of the education system.

Teachers in special education, too, are in a different and often more difficult position than their colleagues in normal education. There has been a good deal of research on teachers, from functional perspectives (Taylor, 1969; Morrison and McIntyre, 1969), conflict perspectives (Grace, 1978) and interaction perspectives (Woods, 1979, 1980b), but teachers in special education have so far been largely ignored by researchers.

Sociologically, this chapter, like previous chapters, remains on a structural level, using conflict perspectives to discuss the relationships between groups in an education system, which have unequal power relationships. The relationship between government and professionals in special education on the one hand, and parents and children on the other, is an illustration of the Weberian point noted in chapter 1 – that dominant interest groups can shape the structures of education for their own purpose. Special education is not shaped and is little influenced by parents. Any participation or involvement of parents is decided upon and implemented by professionals. It is they who, as Sewell has recently pointed out, 'decide which parents can be trusted to be intelligent and not make a fuss' (Sewell, 1981).

Those who control and make decisions in special education also illustrate Lockwood's contention that the powerful must be able to employ ultimate sanctions, for example, legal coercion, but must also be able to prevent opposition arising in the first place, for example, by strategies of persuasion (Lockwood, 1973). Those parents who 'make a fuss' by refusing to allow their child to enter special education or complaining about schools or resources can usually be persuaded to co-operate.

Powerful groups usually develop ideologies which help to legitimate their claims to make decisions about other people. In special education, the ideology of benevolent expertise is very strong. Within this ideology the notion that a child's welfare should rightly be a matter for capable experts has become such a natural assumption that questioning it becomes very difficult. Parents are not supposed to 'know best' about their children's special needs, and those who question their inferior power position can easily be labelled as ungrateful or as a 'problem family'.

Parents

Parental participation

Over the past decade there has been an increasing emphasis on home-school links and parental rights in the education system. This is often expressed in the vocabulary of 'should' and 'ought'. The green paper on education, published in 1977, noted that: 'The government are of the view that parents should be given much more information about schools and should be consulted more widely' (Department of Education and Science, 1977b, p. 5) and in the same year the Taylor Committee wrote that: 'We believe that governing bodies should encourage the widest and deepest parental commitment to the school' (Taylor Report, 1977).

In special education, recent official pronouncements on home-school contacts have moved to the position of not only involving parents, but considering them as partners in the educative processes. Thus Circular 2/75 noted that the use of overt sanctions, the 'certification' procedures, was diminishing and parents were increasingly bringing concern about their handicapped children to the attention of specialists. For the first time in central government recommendations, a statement was made that parents 'should be involved at all stages of the assessment process, their opinions should be sought and their legal rights explained to them. In these ways their morale will be raised and their child should benefit' (Department of Education and Science, 1975a, p. 2).

The Warnock Committee included references to parental involvement throughout their report and concluded:

> We have insisted throughout this report that the successful education of children with special needs is dependent on the full involvement of their parents, indeed, unless parents are seen as equal partners in the educative process the purpose of our report will be frustrated. (*Special Educational Needs* . . ., 1978, p. 150)

But there are problems in bridging the gap between rhetoric and reality. It is important to stress that there is no democratic process within the English state education system which actually helps parents to be equal participants in the educative process, with a right to be involved in educational decisions about their children. Parental rights, under the 1944 and the 1980 and 1981 Education Acts, amount to a grudging appeals system to which few parents will actually have recourse.

Under Section 16 of the 1981 Education Bill the onus is placed on parents to secure the education of their children according to their age, ability, aptitude, and 'to any special needs he may have'. Parents who fail to comply with a local authority notice of assessment of their child may be liable to a fine of up to fifty pounds. Parents whose children are destined to be recorded, or, as the Bill puts it, to have a statement made and maintained on them, may appeal to a special committee (set up under the Education Act 1980), but the decision of this committee need not be binding on the local authority. They may then appeal to the Secretary of State, but, as the experience of this provision in the 1944 Act demonstrated, few parents are willing or knowledgeable enough to pursue the matter to this level. The 1981 Education Bill would seem to be designed to ensure the compliance of the larger number of parents who will now be involved in special education, ultimately under coercive sanction.

The whole ideology of professional expertise denies that parents are competent to make educational decisions about their children. In any event, if a continuum of competence is envisaged, along which professional people place parents, those with handicapped children or children with special needs would probably be placed towards the end of the continuum. The probable incompetence of parents, and their need for help and advice has been stressed so often that many parents accept their 'need' uncritically. Sheridan, delivering the National Convocation lecture in 1965, declared that: 'Parental instinct, however strong and generous, is not infallible . . . expert guidance, can only be given by workers who possess a thorough knowledge of the growth and development of normal children' (Sheridan, 1965).

The attitudes of professionals towards parents have undoubtedly been shaped by the social class position of the clientele with whom they deal. It has already been noted that while the 24 per cent of children in the existing normative categories of handicap cross-cut all social classes, parents – the 76 per cent of those with children in the non-normative categories – are largely from the manual working class. Manual working-class parents have undoubtedly been placed, after the war, in an invidious position in the education system generally. In the education literature the influence of the 'good home' on educational success has been extensively documented, and popular post-Plowden explanations have stressed the supposed failure of manual working-class parents to equip their children with the requisite skills for educational success (Plowden, 1967; Craft, 1970). Add to this the whole history of the concept of 'defect', and the links made in the early twentieth century between defect, disability and a variety of social evils, and it is not surprising that professionals view parents as probably ignorant and incompetent. It is logical, given existing power structures, that professional people will not deem it necessary to consult as equals those whom they consider to be deficient.

However, it could be argued that it is more difficult for professionals to regard middle-class parents as deficient or incompetent. The relationship between professionals and middle-class parents in special education is an interesting and relatively unexplored field. There are indications that there is more dialogue with these parents as they can, and do, form pressure groups and press for resources for their often severely handicapped children. A letter to *Parents Voice*, the journal of the National Society for Mentally Handicapped Children, illustrates this: the writer, an articulate parent with a severely handicapped three-year-old child, gave his advice to other parents thus: 'Challenge the system, challenge the lack of resources, question professionalism and set your sights on the provision you want' (*Parents Voice*, 1978). This kind of advice would be difficult enough for middle-class parents to follow – impossible for working-class parents, who are often less informed and articulate. It is possible, though, for parents occasionally to adopt strategies of refusal and non-compliance which eventually 'defeat' the professionals, as Sewell described in a recent paper (Sewell, 1981).

How does official pronouncement on parental participation match up with reality? A research project carried out for the Warnock Committee found that many parents of handicapped children under five were dissatisfied with the insensitive way in which their child's disability had been revealed to them. They felt they had been given inadequate and confusing information about the nature of the disability and insufficient guidance on how to cope with the child at home (Chazan, Laing, *et al*., 1980). A study by Hunt of 94 parents of ESN children recorded that over half the parents were dissatisfied by the way in which the professionals had treated them, even to the point of not actually explaining that their children were to be moved to a special school. They reported being 'shocked or surprised' on finding this out (Hunt, 1973).

Booth's study of the social process by which a young baby became classified as a handicapped child (Booth, 1978) also noted parental suspicion at what they regarded as professional prevarication, but parents seldom felt competent to question professional judgment.

> When Vicky was ten months old, Mrs Castle noticed she wasn't sitting up properly. She took her to the Health Clinic where she was told that Vicky was just a lazy baby . . .
> Mrs Rymer realised that Stuart was slow in maturing but when she mentioned this fact . . . was told, 'not to worry, he'll catch up'. (Booth, 1978)

This kind of professional prevarication – which, as Booth noted, might very well cloak a clinical undertainty – does lay a basis for mistrust and a feeling that 'they don't tell us anything'.

In the study of ESN-M children carried out in 1976–7 (Tomlinson, 1981), parents did not feel they were sufficiently informed about decisions made by the professionals, their children's disabilities were not explained to them in a manner they could understand, and they felt 'pushed around' by a complex and frustrating system. Even parents who sought help were sometimes embittered by what they saw as the indifference of professionals and their own lack of knowledge as to how to obtain help. As one mother reported,

> I needed help. I had these two handicapped children. I took the bus to town to find the mental health people, what do you do, stand in the town centre and shout 'where are you?' I ended up in tears there and a postman sent me back to my own area office. Next day I put on their coats and went to see Councillor S. and the next day the head of the special school came round.

Putting the rhetoric of parental involvement into practice has largely been concentrated in the area of severe subnormality, with the setting up, in some areas, of parents' workshops. The rationale behind workshops is that from the professional point of view, 'no matter how successfully a child is taught in school, the effort is largely wasted unless systematic steps are taken to help the child to use and apply his knowledge' (Mittler, 1978).

It is assumed that because severely subnormal children need direction, repetition and overlearning of skills, parents must be taught to do this. A parents' workshop was described by Attwood (Attwood, 1977) as one where mothers (rather than parents) attended meetings to listen to talks in child development, behaviour modification and how to observe, and fill in progress charts. From the professional point of view the workshop was a success, the mothers relaxed, and 'the workshop appeared not only to facilitate the learning of specific skills, it helped the parents' emotional adjustment to having a handicapped child'.

An attempt to involve parents of ESN-M children in a workshop was described by Robinson (1979). This teacher described how she equipped herself with counselling skills both to train parents to 'teach' their children at home via Ladybird books and pastry-making, and also to teach the parents some principles of behaviour modification. She concluded that:

> Most find the workshops offer a concrete way of finding out what to do with their child. Moreover, for the child, using the material under a teacher's guidance gives it a credibility it might lack if it appeared to be just something Mum had dreamed up. (Robinson, 1979, p. 14)

The emphasis in both these projects is less on partnership than on professionals instructing parents in how to behave towards their children. There is no suggestion that parents might validly question professional practices. Parents are expected, at best, to be passive partners.

This emphasis of the competence and expertise of professionals to tell mothers how to deal with their children and to structure parents' actions has come in for some criticism. Barton and Moody (1981) have discussed whether parental participation, if structured by the professionals rather than based on any notion of equality, might have more to do with social control than participation. Parents may want to be involved and feel they need help, but if involvement is one-way they may become less enthusiastic. Real participation means that information is shared and parents are not denied knowledge about their children, but it has already been noted that the secretive nature of the special education processes makes this impossible. The 1980 white paper indicated that 'the government agrees with the widely-held view that it would be wrong to require full disclosure to parents of professional reports' (Department of Education and Science, 1980b). Presumably, the widely held view is the professional rather than parental view. If parents have their actions directed by professionals and are denied access to knowledge by professionals, participation may become, at least, more of a matter of subtle manipulation than anything else.

Parents and the assessment process

The ambiguity of the parental position in special education stems from the particular nature of the coercive measures which can be used to ensure that children can be placed in some form of special schooling against the parents' wishes.

While the ideology of government and professionals has been to present special education as a helpful variant of normal education, the reality, as most parents are aware, is to remove children from the credentialling, examination-oriented system. For some parents and children this may be a relief, and the 1944 and the 1980 and 1981 Education Acts allow parents to request assessment and special help for their children. However, enforceable procedures grew out of the recognition that the majority of parents would not wish their child to be placed in special education. When the Wood Committee, reporting in 1929, urged that certification of children should be abolished, the National Union of Teachers argued that the committee were naive to suppose that parents would be as eager for their children to attend special schools as to attend ordinary state schools (National Union of Teachers, 1930).

The statutory involvement and consultation of parents whose children may require special education has always been cursory and occasionally punitive. Under section 34(i) of the 1944 Act, parents who failed to submit their children for a medical examination to ascertain a 'disability of body or mind' were liable to a fine. If a local authority decided that a child needed special education, the only statutory requirement was that they should give the parents notice of their decision. The Handicapped Pupils (HP) forms, used between 1945 and 1975 by most local authorities as part of the procedures by which children were referred and assessed as in need of special education, contained several references to parents, but with little suggestion that they might be caring or responsible people. Parents appeared to be regarded more as objects of possible hindrance in the operation of smooth bureaucratic processes. Thus HP 2 parts 1 and 2 ask the examiner of the child to record important factors of the child's social history, family history or relevant family history, but with no instruction that the person signing the form should actually have visited the home. Part 3 of the form asks for a personal history of the child and 'the examiners' impression of parents . . . if not present, state reasons'. It is difficult to see how the preceding sections could have been adequately completed without parental co-operation. HP 3, the head teacher's form, concluded with a section called 'Additional Information', and a note to the head: 'Here make any observations about the child which appear relevant – his home, family, co-operation of parents with school, etc.'

The special education (SE) forms, which replaced the HP forms after 1975, still contain little suggestion of genuine parental involvement. Nor is there any provision for recording parents' views about the referral and assessment of their children, except at second hand through a professional person's judgment. The suggestion made by the Warnock Report, that parents should be given their own SE form to complete, has not been taken up by the government. Thus, on SE1 the head teacher is required to 'describe the parents' reactions when the child's difficulties were discussed and indicate their likely attitude to any forms of special education that might be called for'. The medical officer, on SE 2, is required to tick section 9, family, social and personal history, only if it is 'normal as far as is known'. The psychologist may complete section 9 of SE 3 'any relevant information about the child's family background and indicate his or her opinion of the attitudes of parents to special education'. The summary form, SE4, which may be filled out by a person who has not seen the parents, includes a simple four-fold classification of parents as either 'supportive, neutral, over-protective, or rejecting' and indicate attitudes to special education as 'in favour, indifferent, unknown, opposed'. It is difficult to equate the official declared policy of parental involvement with a stigmatic characterisation of parents in a simplistic manner. It is worth reiterating here that the judgments of professionals are dependent as much on their own beliefs, values and class position as on any 'objective' knowledge.

In a study of forty ESN-M children (Tomlinson, 1981), all the parents whose children were in or moving into this type of special education were interviewed to elucidate their views on the assessment processes, and their involvement. The majority of parents felt that rather than being consulted about their children's possible learning and behavioural difficulties, they had been 'sent for and told' by the heads of the referring schools. Those few who had intuitively felt, usually by comparison with a neighbour's child or brothers and sisters, that there 'might be something wrong' did not know how to initiate any proceedings. There was some confusion over which professionals had seen their children during the assessment processes; several parents did not know what a psychologist was and few understood the significance of 'IQ' scores. Parents understood the medical nature of assessment more clearly, but were likely to be deferential to the medical mystique. They wanted to be given more medical information about their children, and were confused when doctors introduced educational questions. None of them realised the legal implications of a medical officer seeing their child, and although uneasily aware that there could be an element of compulsion in the procedures, were not clear about its nature or any rights they might have. Parents with school-age children tended to be very dependent on the referring head's presentation of 'what was wrong with the child' and how a 'special school would help', and this dependency eased the head's task of persuasion. Some parents were angry at the idea that their child was being 'kicked out' of normal school, but felt powerless to prevent it. Parents who felt that normal schools 'didn't do their job properly' felt they had no way of making their views known. Parents preferred to think of ESN-M schools as places that could help their children academically – make them literate – and this became a source of some conflict when children did not 'get on better' at special school.

Parents, on the whole, did not feel sufficiently informed about judgments and decisions made about their children. Their child's disabilities or needs were not explained to them in a manner that they could understand, and they felt 'pushed around' by a complex system. Even those parents who actively sought help felt frustrated by what they saw as professional indifference and their own lack of knowledge as to how to obtain help. There is no machinery for adequate parental consultation built into the referral and assessment procedures for special education.

The following three case studies illustrate particular situations that can arise during the assessment processes in which parents are dealt with, or deal with, the professionals. The first case study illustrates the way in which certain parents, pre-judged as incompetent, are not consulted by professionals and the idea of 'equal' involvement is regarded as something of a joke.

> Mrs O'D. has had seven children and is divorced from her second husband. She has the label of being 'well-known to the social services' and lives in a patched council property underneath a raised motorway. She has seven children, one dead, one 'in the reform [school]' and four in care but allowed home at weekends. She lives with her youngest child and wants a bigger house and all her children back. She admits to having a 'terrible temper', but is down on several professional files as having a deep affection for her children. Her ten-year-old son, Teddy, was referred by his primary school for aggressive behaviour when he was eight; the head described him as vindictive and disruptive in class. Although Mrs O'D. had visited the head to complain about other children teasing Teddy, the head decided that the boy had a bad home background and would be better off in a residential school. The psychologist who tested Teddy gave him an IQ score of 69 and eight other tests and decided that 'His response on projective testing reveals a frequent tendency to fantasy, compensation for the unexciting routine which characterises his home circumstances.' He thought Mrs O'D. was a 'bit limited' herself and that the boy was socially disadvantaged. The doctor who examined Teddy also thought the boy was deprived and needed special care and had not consulted the mother. She thought that a single-parent family was a bad environment for the boy. Eventually, Teddy was accepted into a residential ESN-M school. The head of the special school was the only professional to make an attempt to consult with Mrs O'D. – as he put it: 'we worked on the family and the mother is co-operative now'.

The second case study illustrates the way in which professionals may set out to consult and involve parents, but instead manage to confuse them and convince them of their powerlessness.

The Rumfords have four children and live on a pleasant post-war suburban housing estate. They have been 'involved' in special education for seven years, between the referral of their son and his eventual placement in an ESN-M school. Tom had been referred in 1970 as a 'meek little lad' who would benefit from special school, but the parents were not consulted. He remained at normal school until 1973 when he was again referred as an urgent case by the head of his primary school. The head wrote a number of letters to the Rumfords' home, but never visited and they did not visit the school. The parents were, in fact, semi-literate, and disregarded any letters they got from 'the authorities'. Their understanding of the process was that 'they were trying to get the boy away from us'. In 1975 a psychologist finally visited the home to discuss Tom's learning problems and noted that 'at no time has anyone attempted to define a problem or explain why we are trying to get the boy away'. Mrs Rumford had been sent seven letters giving her medical appointments, but only attended after the psychologist suggested that she ought to go. She was surprised that the doctor told her that Tom should go to a special school. She was, in fact, quite willing for the boy to attend special school once it had been explained to her. As she put it, 'They tell us which schools to send the children to, don't they?'

The third case study illustrates the way in which articulate middle-class parents can 'deflect' a decision that they might have an ESN-M child and adopt strategies which overcome professional judgments.

James had been referred by the head of his primary school as a non-reader in 1975, and the psychologist who tested the boy had noted that he came from a good socio-economic and academically advantaged background. The head of the normal school had been hesitant to broach James's problems to the parents and when he did they insisted that the boy should have special remedial help. Despite the psychologist giving the boy an IQ of 67 and recommending special school provision, the parents objected to the idea of ESN-M school in a forceful and articulate manner. They made sufficient 'fuss' in a manner which the professionals found difficult to deal with. After a year, the subject of special school was raised again, but by then the parents had taken the initiative and visited the head of a secondary school who was willing to take James on his transfer from primary school. The parents had a knowledge of the school system and could answer the professionals with an articulate determination, and this no doubt helped to prevent their son becoming an ESN-M child.

Despite this example, middle-class professional people do not generally involve or consult as 'equals', parents whom they associate with incompetency, and since the majority of parents in special education are likely to be working-class, and likely to be associated with incompetence, this may be one of the crucial difficulties in developing adequate involvement of, and consultation with, *all* parents whose children may be considered to be in need of special education.

The projected increase in the numbers of children with special needs mean that more parents will have to be persuaded that these 'needs' exist, and the task of involving parents both in the assessment processes and encouraging participation in actual special education may involve more coercive sanctions, or, as is more likely, the development of new ideologies to rationalise 'special need'.

Pupils

The experience of pupils in special schools

Sociological knowledge about the experiences of children in any type of schooling is severely limited – sociologists of education have only recently begun to focus their work on pupils, in terms of teacher-pupil interaction and pupil re-action to schools. It is the newer sociological perspectives, interpretative and interactionist (Stubbs and Delamonte, 1976; Woods, 1979), and the neo-Marxist conflict approaches (Sharp and Green, 1973; Willis, 1977) which have come closest to describing the experiences of children, through observation and interview, and tried to relate the micro-experiences of the classroom world to the macro-world of the wider social structure. It is generally accepted among sociologists of education that while interactionist studies have broadened an understanding of school activities and processes, and provided some conceptual and methodological tools for analysis of what actually goes on in school, it is conflict approaches which have attempted to explain school processes within the wider society, examining the ways in which the processes can act as forms of social control, or of social and cultural reproduction. Weberian approaches, too, have proved useful in analysing what teachers and pupils actually do in schools. King's (1978) study of an infant school focused on the interests and ideologies of teachers and how these ideologies held by the teachers actually constrained their actions and their views on the potential of the children they taught.

Sociological understanding of the experiences and opinions of children moving into or in special education is totally lacking. It is probably a reflection of the hierarchical value placed on different types of schools in our society that studies noting the reactions of pupils were first undertaken in public school (Wakeford, 1969) and grammar school (Lacey, 1967) with one study of secondary modern school (Hargreaves, 1967) and one of comprehensive (Ford, 1969) emerging in the 1960s. Studies of primary and middle schools did not appear until the 1970s and presumably it will be the 1980s before sociologists arrive in special schools.

This lack of information is particularly distressing at a time of official change and government intervention in special education, as it is largely through an understanding of how special school pupils experience their schooling that any evaluation as to whether their special needs are being met can be made, particularly since more conventional evaluation in terms of academic attainment is often not possible. Likewise, it is largely by examining teacher-pupil interaction and special school processes that we can raise pertinent questions about the nature and purpose of special education.

The experiences of children in all types of special schools, units and classes are radically different from those of children in normal schools, despite attempts to blur the distinction by claiming that special education is merely a helpful variant of normal education. But the experiences of pupils with different kinds of handicap or need in existing types of special schools may appear to be so diffuse that no generalisations can be made. For example, the experience of a spastic-deaf child in a school for the physically handicapped, or a blind pupil in one of the grammar schools for the blind,[1] or a mildly educationally subnormal child in an inner-city area will obviously be different in a variety of ways. Also the experiences of children in what I have called the non-normative categories may very well be different from those in the normative categories since, as we have noted, the 'special needs' of the non-normative have as much to do with the perception of teachers and other professionals as with 'needs'.

However, there are three ways in which generalisations can be made about the experience of all children in special schools. First, by referring to the legal aspects of special education; second, by pointing to the negative emphasis and low educational status of special schools; and third, by noting the relative powerlessness of the children.

Legally, children within special education are in a different situation to those in normal education. Special education is the only form of education where a child who has not been before the courts may be placed in a particular type of school against his or her parents' wishes. This takes the matter away from an educational aegis and places it under one of civil rights, as American experiences of legal action over special education have demonstrated (Weatherley and Lipsky, 1977). There is little possibility that a child can experience special education as a helpful variant of normal education if he or she is experiencing it under threat of compulsion. The legal position laid down by the 1944 Education Act has been superseded by the 1980 Education Act and by new legislation. Under the terms of the 1980 white paper, children already ascertained as requiring special education, and those progressing beyond stage 3 of assessment procedures, will be recorded and the LEA will 'maintain a statement' on them.

Parents of these children will have a right to appeal against recording to a local authority appeals committee, established by the 1980 Act. But the LEA will be able to ignore the decision of the appeals committee, as 'the committee's findings will not be binding on the LEA but will be in the nature of a recommendation' (Department of Education and Science, 1980b, p. 19). For the 'non-recorded' children – those who do not progress beyond stage three of the assessment processes, and who will mainly fall

into the non-normative categories of ESN-M maladjusted, remedial and disruptive – the white paper states that the arrangements
governing choice of school and school attendance procedures
established by the 1980 Education Act will apply. However, a
reading of this act establishes that the section on school attendance orders contains Section 10(5) which states that 'the forego-
ing provision of this section does not apply to children who are in
need of special education' (1980 Education Act).

Parents of non-recorded children in special education will *not*
have the same rights as those with children in normal education,
and parents of recorded children will be subject to quite specific
legally enforceable procedures.

Similarly the arrangements under Section 8 of the 1980 Act
concerning the publication of arrangements for the admission of
children to schools 'do not apply to special schools or children in
need of special educational treatment' (Sect. 9 (2), 1980 Education Act). Children in any type of special education can be thus
contrasted as a group, in terms of their legal position, with children in normal education. Their experiences will be affected by
the coercive nature of the enforceable procedures which lie
behind their arrival in special education. Given the historical
stigma and the new connotations of the term 'special', it is unlikely
that parents, future employers or the pupils themselves will consider that special education is simply a helpful variant having
parity of esteem with normal education.

Children in special education are also affected by the peculiar
negative emphasis of special schooling. The processes of discovery and assessment have an inbuilt negative aspect in that they
concentrate on separating the normal from the not-normal. To
be special is to have the negative attribute of being not-normal.
Once in special education, the processes will stress, explicitly or
implicitly, the negative aspects bound up with handicap or needs
– the *in*capacity, *in*ability or *dis*ability. Just as professionals seldom
regard as equals those parents whom they regard as incompetent,
so teachers in special schools are even less likely to regard their
pupils as agents to be consulted or involved in their own education. Historically, special school pupils have had various unpleasant attributes associated with them, socially, morally and educationally. As Alice Descoeudres wrote in one of the first systematic
practitioners' handbooks on the education of defective children,

'each pupil is . . . a poor little creature who is morally and intellectually inferior to his fellows' (Descoeudres, 1928).

Teaching inferior children, with all the negative aspects attributed to them, was, as Descoeudres also noted, 'a disagreeable task. Teachers of the mentally defective must have sufficiently lofty moral and social ideals not to be repelled by the wearisome, dull and discouraging parts of the work' (Descoeudres, 1928, Preface).

Special school education has always been accorded more negative than positive attributes, even to the negative financial extent of paying special school teachers less, a situation which existed until the Second World War. But the major negative aspect of special schooling is associated with the academic status of the schools. In terms of the examination-oriented values of modern industrial society, everything about most special curricula is negative. No high-status knowledge is imparted, even the basic knowledge which constitutes the primary school curriculum — literacy, numeracy and a preparation for a subject-oriented secondary schooling is not necessarily a part of special schooling, and even the 'low-status' knowledge that some sociologists have observed being imparted in comprehensive schools (Keddie, 1970) is often not available in special schools. What is offered in special schools is frequently non-knowledge in ordinary educational terms.

The third way in which all special children may experience their schooling is in terms of their powerlessness. Although children in normal schools may be at the bottom of any hierarchies of power, there are ways in which special school children are more completely on the 'receiving end' of school processes than children in normal schools. Children may be subject, literally, to more physical supervision by teachers. Some handicapped children will be physically moved around by teachers and assistants, non-ambulant children will depend on technical and human aid, and there may be more physical restraint of children who are disruptive or aggressive. The children will have less opportunity to 'complain' about their treatment, in that, having already been judged as not-normal, their reactions may be ignored or elicit less response from parents, teachers and others than the complaints or reactions of children in normal schools.

Pupil control

The experience of children in special schools is most consistently related to control. Indeed, as the next chapter demonstrates, control has always been an explicit goal of much special schooling, although currently expressed more in terms of social adjustment, or social training.

Although control expressed in terms of discipline and efficiency was a characteristic of state elementary schooling from its inception, control in special schools was particularly carefully monitored. An inspector's report for one special school at the beginning of the century read: '9/1/1900 – The efficient conduct of this class has been fully maintained during the past year, – the children are satisfactorily taught according to their peculiarities and progress duly noted. The discipline is good and the children appear to be happy' (quoted in Spragg, 1976). Punishment recorded in this particular school read as follows:

1/7/1908	*Offence*	Threatening and kicking a teacher
	Punishment	Several strokes with hand and dry bread for dinner
1/6/1910	*Offence*	Repeatedly going off after free breakfast
	Punishment	Several strokes
1/11/1910	*Offence*	Moving out of desk and walking round room
	Punishment	Two strokes
1/10/1913	*Offence*	Impudence
	Punishment	A good shaking
2/11/1924	*Offence*	Indecent note to a girl
	Punishment	Two strokes on each hand

The problem of control has thus always been very important in special education, particularly in the majority of special schools, that is, those containing ESN or maladjusted children, but the ways in which control is currently implemented may be more subtle than earlier in the century, particularly since the advent of psychological, psychotherapeutic and counselling practices. For example, a psychologically-oriented social skill training programme for maladjusted boys was recently described by Curtis (1980).

The boys were to be taught social skills, defined as 'the ability to interact with others in a given social context in specific ways which are socially acceptable or valued and at the same time personally beneficial'.

The assumption behind the teaching, which made extensive use of video-recordings for the boys to watch their own behaviour, was that 'emotional and psychological life-coping skills, as well as academic skills, need to be taught'. In one case, Edward, who usually exhibited inappropriate 'grinning, giggling and a loud wah', was shown by video that he could behave better. Although this particular programme only used 'suggestion' to change behaviour, this kind of approach illustrates a collection of practices, originally derived from the behaviourist tradition in psychology (Skinner, 1953) which have become known as behaviour modification.

The whole area of behaviour modification in special education, particularly the uncritical acceptance of ill-understood practices, is one of the areas that could well be subject to sociological critique. As Strivens has recently pointed out (Strivens, 1981), debates between psychologists over the uses of behaviour modification techniques may stress eclecticism and the ability of the child to make choices (Meichenbaum, 1976; Bandura, 1977), but do little to address the issue as to how far behaviour modification is a form of social control, given the unequal power relationship between those 'modifying' the behaviour of children and young people. The crucial questions as to who defines appropriate behaviour, and who has the power to give or withhold resources or rewards until appropriate behaviour is produced, are seldom discussed in the behaviour modification literature. Likewise, as Strivens points out, it is particularly necessary for practitioners to reflect on 'why certain skills are regarded as "appropriate" '.

It has already been noted that physical control, in terms of moving children around, or constraining their actions, is more readily acceptable in special schools. Paradoxically, though, 'bad' behaviour may be tolerated more. Many children in special education are expected to behave badly, in ways that normal schools may not permit. Their troublesome behaviour may, after all, be one reason for their exclusion from normal education. There is, in special schools, less pressure to control children so that other, academic, goals can be achieved. However, control does remain a major problem in special schooling and the forms that it takes will depend on teacher ideologies and beliefs in particular schools, and particularly on the head teacher. The following case study illustrates the attempts of one school to meet the challenge of disruption. The case was recorded during a day of observation at an ESN-M school,[2] one in which the head teacher's declared commitment was to a 'therapeutic community'.

Jimmy – a case study

A.M. Jimmy, a West Indian boy of eleven, came to school on time with a guide, and sat quietly in assembly. In his classroom he did not settle to the work Mr B. gave him – tracing his name on a printed sheet – and wandered around and out into the corridor. Mr B., whose policy it is to allow wandering, remonstrated quietly with him. Eventually, Jimmy wandered into a neighbouring class, snatched some sweets from a child and ran back into the corridor. Mrs C., in whose class the incident happened, sent four children out to take the sweets back from Jimmy. Enraged, he ran back into the classroom, where Mrs C. and her assistant grabbed him, pushed him out and locked the door. Even more furious, Jimmy rushed out of the school, round to Mrs C.'s room and broke her classroom window with a piece of wood. Two male teachers were called to bring Jimmy back into school, whereupon he ran back into the corridor, grabbed a hammer from a work bench and threatened the teachers. The head was called to talk to him; he eventually calmed down and went willingly into the head's room.

P.M. The main topic of the after-school staff meeting was the Jimmy incident. The head introduced the topic, saying, 'We have to discuss this, as the Jimmies are our biggest challenge. How do we control them? Particularly if they operate an extortion racket by taking sweets.' Two staff came to Jimmy's defence; Mrs M. pointed out that, as usual, Jimmy had had no breakfast and was badly behaved when hungry, and Mr B. asked the staff to remember that Jimmy was partially deaf, but had been thrown out of the deaf unit that he originally attended for bad behaviour. Other staff suggested that the boy should be sent back to the deaf unit, but the head said no, it was impossible, 'deaf schools are loath to take ESN children'. Other suggestions for meeting the challenge of the Jimmies were as follows: exclude the boy from school, try to get another ESN school to accept him, ask the educational psychologist for a programme of behaviour modification, or a 'recourse to chemistry' (drugs). One teacher was of the opinion that 'Old Testament punishment was the best' and a good beating was the answer. Mrs C. and her assistant complained that the boy was strong and violent and they couldn't hold him down, and the head said he would discuss the boy with the visiting psychiatrist.

> *Observer's note* I interpreted the Jimmy incident as being
> initially Mrs C.'s fault – she and her assistant did not appear
> to be very competent dealing with any of the children. If
> Jimmy was hungry it was logical of him to take the sweets –
> could they have found some food to offer him? Ask for the
> sweets back themselves, rather than sending other children?
> Why lock him out? What kind of response was he supposed to
> come up with? Would it have been better if Mr B. had insisted
> on his remaining in his own classroom to work?

The judgments of outside observers as to whether participants in a social situation should or should not have acted differently are not, of course, sociological. A sociological analysis of the Jimmy incident could ask questions about teacher-pupil interaction in terms of teacher survival strategies (Woods, 1980b). How do teachers actually cope and survive in dealing with wandering, disruptive or aggressive children, and how far does their choice of strategies depend on their prior beliefs and ideologies. The different reactions to the 'challenge of the Jimmies' certainly illustrated a variety of beliefs on which action could be taken. But the challenge of control in school is certainly related to the wider social structure. The children in ESN-M schools, as we have noted, are the children of manual working-class parentage, with an over-representation of black children; the measures taken to control these children in schools are related to the relatively powerless position of these social and racial groups outside school.

The 'recourse to chemistry' suggested by one teacher in the Jimmy incident referred to the possibility of using drugs to control aggressive behaviour. While in the context of prison drug therapy has recently been subject to critical scrutiny (*The Times*, 25 October 1980b), there has been little comment on the use of drugs in special education generally.[3] Medical dominance in special education and the accepted medical treatment of some normative, organic defects meant that the shift to controlling non-organic conditions, such as behaviour that had been judged deviant by, drug therapy, was relatively easily accomplished, and the extent to which drugs are used in special schools is unknown. It is here that the distinction between normative and non-normative categories of handicap or 'need' becomes crucial. As Box noted, in an article entitled 'Hyperactivity – the Scandalous Silence':

> Children are no longer naughty, they are medical cases. With this re-conceptualisation of the problem, American schools, particularly in poor Negro ghettos, and English schools in urban slums and ethnically mixed areas, are being transformed from places where children attended educational courses to where they receive courses in medical treatment. (Box, 1977)

Box's article was received with some hostility (*New Society*, 8 December 1977) and he certainly overstated his case, but observation in ESN schools can confirm that drugs can be used to 'quieten children down'. This kind of medical control of social and moral behaviour does raise a variety of questions concerning the function and purpose of special schooling. It should perhaps be noted in passing that there may be differences in the nature of control adopted in residential and day special schooling. A good deal of special education, particularly for handicaps or needs judged to be more severe, takes place in residential institutions in which the pupils may be subject to specific kinds of control and have fewer strategies of resistance.

Pupil response

Pupils in special schools are no more 'empty vessels to be filled, nor pieces of clay to be pressed into shape' (Woods, 1980b, Introduction) than pupils in ordinary schools, but pupils' response in special education is a product of their own special situation. The powerlessness of pupils in special education leads to a high degree of frustration. They have little choice in their own schooling, not being consulted during the assessment processes, and they have little freedom to choose school activities or to withdraw from them. The closer supervision of special school children in terms of transport and guides who bring them to school, means that there is literally less chance of them truanting or choosing not to attend school. Many special school pupils are acutely aware of the low status of their schooling and the fact that they cannot be demoted any further in the education process, and they are at a disadvantage in being taken seriously if they complain about their special schooling. Criticism or hostile reaction can easily be dismissed as a child being 'not normal' or 'acting out his problems'. The case of Albert W. illustrates a boy who was attending an ESN-M school against his own and his parents' wishes. He had definite opinions on his schooling and ambitions for his future which were unlikely to be listened to or taken seriously by the school.

> Albert was the fifth child in a family well-known to the social services. His father was a settled Irish tinker who was permanently unemployed and his eldest sister and three brothers had all attended special schools. Albert had arrived in the remedial department of his secondary school only to be referred with five other boys as possibly in need of special education. The psychologist who saw and tested all the boys described him as the worst of the referrals, although his IQ score was given as 80, and contacted the head of the special school that Albert's brothers had attended, although there was a school nearer. The school was one which was concerned about falling rolls, the head agreed to take the boy quickly and he was admitted without a medical examination. The school did not have a high opinion of him; they regarded him as 'remedial and delinquent rather than ESN' and described him as a petty pilferer with an inflated opinion of himself and a low tolerance of frustration. When seen at home, Albert's opinions about the school were equally uncomplimentary. He thought it was 'a dump where they pushed you around'. He felt he had been getting on all right in the remedial department of his secondary school, and brought out some work he had done there – a project on the army. He said he

would like to join the army when he left school but knew that the army didn't take boys from ESN schools. This was a major reason for dislike of the ESN school, and of the frustration he felt that he was forced to attend.

There could be, of course, cases where children were happy to be in special schooling, and, if consulted, could offer constructive suggestions as to how to improve facilities.

The treatment of parents and children in special education as equal participants would seem to be a highly unlikely situation, given prevailing professional ideologies, and special education is certainly not structured with client response or satisfaction in mind.

Teachers

Teachers in special education

It would, nevertheless, be wrong to assume that special school teachers can exert unconstrained influence over parents and children. In common with their colleagues in normal education, their autonomy is more often myth than reality – they are constrained in a variety of ways, and their day-to-day actions are often the product of pragmatic necessary strategies for survival in what are often very difficult situations.

It has already been noted, in chapter 4, that within the occupational group of teachers as a whole, special school teachers have historically been regarded until quite recently as a lower-status sub-group. The history of teacher recruitment generally (Floud and Scott, 1961; Grace, 1978) demonstrates a sharp divergence between public and grammar school teachers, and the elementary school teachers who were recruited mainly from the children of skilled manual workers and the 'lower' middle class. During the later twentieth century the relatively higher status accorded to graduate teachers of 'high-ability' children and the lower status accorded to the old secondary-modern-type teacher has created what Hargreaves has described as an 'uncomfortable alliance . . . in the staffrooms of many comprehensive schools' (Hargreaves, 1980, p. 129).

Within this uncomfortable alliance of traditional grammar-type, subject-oriented teachers of higher-ability children, and primary- and secondary-modern-type teachers, special school teachers are firmly allied to the latter. This has to do with origins and professional identity. Special school teachers were, from the 1890s, recruited from those elementary school teachers who, for a variety of reasons, chose to 'cope with defective children' (Lindsey, 1957), and, as Descoeudres wrote, 'were at once met with expressions of sympathy, mingled at times with shades of pity' (Descoeudres, 1928, Preface). In a league table of status, remuneration, qualifications and other trappings of professionalism, special school teachers have usually been at the bottom. The identity and occupational culture (Hargreaves, 1980) of special school teachers is also firmly shaped by pedagogical practice and expertise, rather than subject-orientation. They can 'deal' with the defective, the handicapped or those with special needs.

Nevertheless, there has always been a movement to create and develop a 'special' professional autonomy. Special school teachers had formed an association and produced their own journal by 1903[4] and by 1922 the National Union of Teachers had created a special education section. Although originally fragmented by the feeling that teachers of different types of handicap had little in common and by the proliferation of organisations and pressure groups formed around various types of handicap (see Segal, 1974, for some of these), special school teachers had, certainly by the later 1970s, realised that their common interests lay in unification to enhance their professional claims to the special expertise which would bring status, respect and guaranteed occupation. The claims to possess a special expertise have been strengthened, rather than weakened, by the possibilities of integration; the expansion of special teaching outside the special school has created the possibility of more expert advisors to deal with more children designated as having special needs. Indeed, the Warnock Report devoted a whole chapter to 'advice and support in special education' (*Special Educational Needs* . . ., 1978, ch. 13) in which the 'expertise of specialist teachers' would provide more specialist jobs.

Qualifications and training

Enhancement of professional status in a society in which qualifications are being progressively upgraded has meant that special school teachers must be seen to possess special qualifications, and this enhancement certainly has support from government as expressed in the Warnock Report and the 1980 white paper. A proposal put forward by the National Advisory Council on the Training and Supply of Teachers in 1954 – that all special school teachers should have special qualifications – was never implemented, but the Warnock Report in 1978 accepted the principle that 'all teachers with defined responsibilities for children with special educational needs, wherever they are receiving education, should have an additional qualification in special education' (*Special Educational Needs* . . ., 1978, p. 234), and the white paper considered that teacher ability to recognise and deal with special needs should be reflected in teacher training (Department of Education and Science, 1980b, p. 11). The familiar proviso that this should not cost too much can also be noted in the white paper.

It was not, however, until 1959 that the handicapped pupils and special school regulations required all teachers in special schools in England and Wales to have even an ordinary teaching qualification. In schools for the blind, deaf and partially hearing, in which teachers were required to have a further qualification, by 1977, only 57 per cent of teachers of the blind, 67 per cent of teachers of the deaf, and 74 per cent of teachers of the partially hearing had obtained such a qualification. The 1970 Education (Handicapped Children) Act, which brought severely subnormal children into education, also brought in numbers of unqualified teachers – a situation which over the past ten years has created a variety of conflicts concerned as much with professional status as with teaching ability.[5]

By 1978 the qualifications of special school teachers were approximately as follows: 2,594 graduates and 15,716 non-graduates, giving a total of 18,310, of whom 4,028 (22 per cent) had additional qualifications (adapted from *Department of Education and Science, Statistics in Education: Teachers*, 1977 and the Warnock Report, *Special Educational Needs* . . ., 1978).

The Warnock Report certainly gave an impetus to training colleges and Institutions of Higher Education to create and develop further courses, both pre- and in-service, to provide a special education qualification. The Report recommended a range of additional qualifications, the requirement of an additional qualification for those with 'defined responsibility for children with special needs' (*Special Educational Needs* . . ., 1978, p. 236), and separate courses to train teachers for the majority of children to be found in special education – those with moderate learning difficulties, that is, the current ESN-M and remedial children. However, there is little evidence to date that these new courses will contain more critical analyses of what currently passes for special education or that they will inject a historical understanding of the social, political and economic events that underlie current debates and changes in special education. Indeed, a review of some revamped courses in 1980[6] suggests that most courses have changed their titles to incorporate the words special needs rather than handicap, and are offering more of the same mixture of psychological theory and pedagogical practice.

Teacher constraints and powers

A critical awareness of what they are actually doing should ideally be a part of the training of all teachers who will in the future teach children designated as having special educational needs. It has already been noted earlier in this chapter that teachers in special education are in a different situation to their colleagues in normal education; in some ways they are subject to fewer constraints and have more immediate power over the pupils. With the removal of academic goals one of the major pressures on teachers in normal schools, that of 'keeping control' so that academic work can continue, is minimised. A major strain on the teachers is thus removed. Certain behaviour is tolerated in special schools and classes that would not be permissible in normal schools. Part of this tolerance stems from the premise that the children have already been judged as deviant, bad or not-normal. The child's 'bad' behaviour becomes a normal attribute and the teacher is partially absolved from making the pupil conform. Similarly, the child's defects, both intellectual and behavioural, can exonerate the teacher if bad behaviour continues. As Descoeudres put it some time ago: 'Those of us who deal with mentally defective children have to realise that their anti-social conduct is a direct result of a lack of understanding rather than moral turpitude' (Descoeudres, 1928).

As the case of Jimmy, quoted earlier in this chapter, demonstrates, the 'bad' behaviour of this pupil called forth a variety of suggestions for dealing with the behaviour, but the teachers felt exonerated from responsibility that they or the school might have shaped the pupil behaviour. Similarly, constraints in the shape of complaints by parents need not, as the section on parents demonstrates, be taken too seriously.

Teachers in special education do have more power over their pupils than other teachers, and much of this power is legitimated by the ideology of benevolent humanitarianism which has allowed the community at large to assume that whatever special school teachers do, it is 'for the good' of the children. The teachers themselves have also managed to keep much of their activity away from public scrutiny. However, there are indications that this situation is changing, and more accountability will be demanded. This may be particularly true in the area of curriculum, to which we now turn.

Chapter Six · The curriculum in special schools

At the heart of a sociological analysis of special education must lie a consideration of the special school curriculum. For it is here that beliefs that the special needs of children are being met can be tested, clarified and appraised by an examination of what teachers and pupils actually do in special schools and classes. For this, information should be available on the goals, aims and objectives of special education, on what counts as a special curriculum, what kinds of knowledge and skills are offered or withheld, what activities are organised, what provision and resources are available, what methods are used, and what types of evaluation are employed. Special needs in themselves do not generate a curriculum.

There is a large literature on practice and method in special schools, with an emphasis on what to teach, and how to teach it. This is particularly true of the literature on the 'slow learner' (Tansley and Gulliford, 1960; Cleugh, 1961; Bell, 1970; Williams, 1970; Brennan, 1974; Brennan, 1979). It is also true of the literature on the severely mentally handicapped, particularly that produced since the DES Education Pamphlet no. 60, *Educating Mentally Handicapped Children* (1975b) (see for example Stevens, 1976; Leeming *et al*., 1979). Much of this literature is 'practitioners talking to each other' – that is, the emphasis is on what to do, rather than on any theoretical consideration as to why it is done. Much of what practitioners and their advisors talk about is classroom practice, provision of resources, and teaching methods – aims, objectives and evaluation are mentioned less often and there is virtually no discussion of the overall goals of special education and the values and beliefs that might be implicit in these goals. Special school teachers, like teachers in other parts of the education system, usually go about their work on a pragmatic

day-to-day basis. Indeed, much of the teacher's activity is dominated by an ethic of practicality. 'The teacher who has fundamen-
tal doubts about his rights to teach the curriculum is at best
regarded as a crank' (Eggleston, 1977, p. 11). But like other
teachers, special school teachers are involved, whether they ack-
nowledge it or not, in issues of power and control, and their
decisions about what comprises the curriculum in their classes do
affect the immediate and future lives of their pupils.

As an example of this power: in a society in which an increasing
amount and complexity of knowledge is needed to function as an
independent person, one implicit goal of special education is to
select out and withhold large amounts of what is generally considered by the rest of society to be important knowledge. If challenged, this selection and withholding may be justified on the
grounds that the children 'cannot benefit', 'would not understand', or have 'special needs'.

Sociologists have, by and large, taken little interest in the curriculum in normal schools, and none at all in the special school
curriculum, and, as Eggleston has pointed out, this has meant
that a study of the curriculum has lacked an adequate consideration of either the social forces that influence it and the social
implications of deciding what curriculum to offer to different
social groups (Eggleston, 1977). It is a truism that every society
makes different kinds and amounts of knowledge available to
different categories of people and it has become a sociological
truism that there are high- and low-status areas of knowledge,
and that academic-type knowledge has a higher status than manual or manipulative skills (Young, 1971; Bernstein, 1975).

'The curriculum', as Musgrave (1972) has noted, 'stands analyt-
ically at the centre of the process whereby any society manages its
stock of knowledge.' It is the distribution of different kinds of
knowledge and skill through the curriculum to different groups
of children or the withholding of certain kinds of knowledge that
largely determines their future status, social and occupational, in
society. Those who are involved in curriculum decisions thus
have great power.

The special school curriculum has probably escaped sociological scrutiny for two reasons. First, it appears to be negatively
defined. It offers 'non-knowledge' in that children who are
offered a special curriculum have already been defined as not

able to benefit from even the low-status knowledge of a normal curriculum. Thus, it seemed self-evident that what goes on in special schools has no relevance to major sociological concerns such as stratification and class. It is a taken-for-granted assumption that most special children would naturally be offered a curriculum consisting of academic non-knowledge and would therefore be outside sociological preoccupations with social equality and social mobility.

Second, the benevolent humanitarianism implicit in the rhetoric of providing special educational treatment for special needs makes it very difficult to subject the special school curriculum to critical scrutiny. The major perspective on the special school curriculum is a philosophical one, a major contributor to this perspective being Mary Warnock, both in her own writings (Warnock, 1977, 1979) and through the Warnock Report. Here education is depoliticised, it is described as 'good . . . to which all human beings are entitled' (*Special Education Needs . . .*, 1978, p. 6), and any criticisms are expressed in terms of failure to specify immediate objectives, and to provide resources. Humanitarian and philosophical approaches make it difficult to enquire who has the power and expertise to decide what form the 'good' shall take, who controls the special school curriculum, and what its ultimate aims are, and who can give or withhold resources.

The Warnock Committee were, in fact, critical of what they saw of the special school curriculum during their collection of evidence:

> While . . . we were impressed by the concern shown for individual pupils . . . we also became aware that the quality of education offered to them is in some respects less satisfactory. (*Special Educational Needs*, p. 205)

> The evidence presented to us reflected a widespread belief that many special schools underestimate their pupil capabilities. This view was expressed in relation to all levels of ability and disability. Many people thought the curriculum was too narrow. (p. 208)

Indeed, the committee were concerned enough over the state of the special school curriculum to recommend that a special section of the Schools Council[1] should be formed and given resources to carry out curriculum projects *and* translate these into forms which could be useful in special schools, units or classes.

This chapter is concerned with an examination of the aims of the special curriculum, noting the overriding aims of training for self-sufficiency and social control of troublesome pupils, and with an examination of accountability and control in special education, particularly stressing the autonomous development of the special school curriculum. The chapter also discusses the curriculum for slow learners in terms of the way in which it can easily reproduce the pupils as low-status, semi- or unskilled workers or unemployable. Initially, an attempt is made to define the special curriculum in terms of the model that most special school teachers appear to employ.

The nature of the special school curriculum

While definitions of curriculum are legion and often unsatisfactory, two definitions present it as concerned with knowledge and learning activities, but set within a social context.

Eggleston (1977, p. 13) considers that curriculum is 'concerned with the presentation of knowledge and involves a pattern of learning experiences . . . Curriculum involves a number of components, including aims, content, methodology, timing and evaluation, that spring, like the curriculum itself, from the normative and power systems of the society.' Lawton (1975, p. 6) writes that: 'the school curriculum is essentially a selection from the culture of a society. Certain aspects of our way of life, certain kinds of knowledge, certain attitudes and values are regarded as so important that their transmission to the next generation is not left to chance.'

Both Eggleston and Lawton refer to hidden curriculum, first referred to by Jackson (1968) – those unofficial, informal activities which count as learning, but which would not appear on a timetable – for example, the learning of implicit standards of appropriate behaviour. This is particularly important in special education, as often what goes on in special school might bear little resemblance to the passing over of knowledge, and is often defined more in terms of social skills and the modification of behaviour. In much of special education, the hidden curriculum of normal schools *becomes* the curriculum of special schools.

Yet whether the curriculum is explicit or hidden, both Eggleston and Lawton would stress that whatever counts as curriculum is not a political entity set apart from the rest of society. The selection from culture, the aims, methods and knowledge chosen for particular groups of children, depend on which particular dominant groups in education with their own ideologies and traditions have the power to make the decisions and provide the resources. It is, as Lawton pointed out in a more recent book (Lawton, 1979), a crucial political question to ask who selects what goes on the curriculum and what methods shall be used.

The Warnock Committee, in its consideration of the curriculum, was not interested in raising these kinds of questions. The committee defined the special school curriculum in terms of a means-end model[2] which most special school teachers, in common with many teachers in normal schools, are likely to be using, implicitly if not explicitly. Thus, to some special school teachers, at least, a model of the curriculum might appear thus:

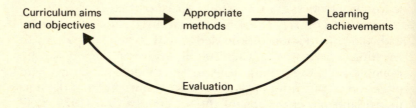

Figure 6.1   (Adapted from Eggleston, 1977, p. 121)

This is, of course, presupposing that the teachers are basing their activities on some kind of a formal means-end model. At worst, special school teaching can easily become child-minding, or supervising random play activities. The Warnock Committee had little to say on the aims of special education. 'The term curriculum as we use it here therefore means those school activities which set out to achieve specific aims within the general aims of education as a whole' (*Special Educational Needs* . . ., 1978, p. 205), and they concentrated on elaborating the means-ends model; that setting of objectives, choice of materials or experiences, choice of methods and appraisal of the effectiveness of achieving objectives were the crucial elements in the development of a special school curriculum.[3]

Much of the literature documenting and criticising special school curricula is expressed in terms of teacher failure to clarify aims, specify objectives, choose appropriate methods and make records so that evaluation can take place. Leeming *et al.* (1979), in their study of ESN-S teachers, wrote that:

> Our own observation of teachers in the classroom led us at first to think that the teachers' approach to the curriculum was conceived at the activity level; and few thought in terms of a philosophy of education from which aims and teaching content could be derived. There seemed to be a total acceptance by teachers of the activities on the timetable rather than questioning what they did and what it achieved for the children (p. 45),

and Brennan's study of the curriculum for slow-learners found that teachers expressed aims in very general terms and that 'in most schools there was a lack of clear understanding that statements of curricula aims are made in a philosophical-ethical frame of reference and require translation into descriptions of pupil behaviour' (Brennan, 1979, p. 68).

Brennan's study was also particularly critical of record-keeping and evaluation in the project schools and was politely lukewarm about the quality of the curriculum offered to slow learners.

Special school practitioners are themselves more anxious now to clarify the nature of the special school curriculum. At an NCSE conference in 1980, Williams commented that 'The question – what is the special education curriculum? – is going to be asked much more frequently in the future. People will be turning to those who claim to have definable responsibilities for children with special needs for an answer.' He also suggested that the special school curriculum would be 'one of the most critical topics of the next decade' (Williams, 1980, pp. 17–19).

It is not particularly surprising that special school teachers should be confused as to the nature of the special school curriculum and its aims and objectives. They operate within an ambiguous frame of reference. On the one hand, they are aware that the children they teach have been categorised out of normal education and away from the aims considered appropriate for normal school children, while on the other, official statements urge them to embrace the same aims as normal schools. Thus the DES pamphlet 60 stated that 'the inclusion of mentally handicapped children within the education system implies broadly common aims for all children' (Department of Education and Science, 1975b).

But this presupposes that there *is* agreement on common curriculum aims for all children, and as recent controversy about curriculum aims has demonstrated (Cox and Dyson, 1969; Cox and Boyson, 1977; Kogan, 1978; Lawton, 1979) there *is* little agreement on broadly common curriculum aims for all children. Where there is agreement, the aims are so general that they have little intrinsic meaning.

In normal schools there is, in fact, little agreement over whether curriculum planning should be aimed at the need to supply trained manpower for industry, or to educate for 'leisure' or possible unemployment – whether to educate an elite few in a high-status academic curriculum or whether a common-core curriculum should be followed for all children in all normal schools. There is even less agreement on whether education should be aimed at providing credentials or providing access to a richer, more worthwhile life. If there is disagreement and controversy over the nature of the curriculum in normal schooling, it is not surprising that there should be disagreement over the nature of the special school curriculum.

The aims of special schooling

There are, however, two ways in which the aims thought appropriate for normal school children and for special school children have overlapped. These are the aims of training pupils for self-sufficiency and productivity, and the aim of producing controlled, moral, social behaviour. These aims presuppose that elite groups with power and influence who have received a superior education can decide on aims for those in mass education, and, indeed, the historical development of the normal elementary school curriculum post-1870 posited mass education concerned with basic literacy, moral training and vocational orientation (Eggleston, 1977, p. 31).

The aim of the pre-twentieth-century education of the blind, deaf, crippled and 'educable imbeciles' was largely concerned with vocational training and the inculcation of some kind of occupational skill to prevent the 'great torrent of pauperism' foreseen by the Egerton Commission (1889; see also chapter 2). In this the aim of special education has always been broadly similar to that for 'normal' working-class children. But even the low-status knowledge of the 'three Rs' offered in elementary schools was eventually considered to be less important for children in special education, particularly for the large group of educable defective children. During the first half of the twentieth century in England, the aims of special education moved away from the 'three Rs' to the 'three Ms' – mechanical or manual, manipulative, and moral training.[4] This latter particularly included an emphasis on celibacy and non-contact with the opposite sex, as the eugenics movement became more influential (see Tredgold and Soddy, 1956, pp. 405 and 437).

The Royal Commission of 1908 was especially preoccupied with debating how much education in basic literacy special school children should receive and noted that

> the drift of opinion favours the extension of manual or industrial training in special school. Manual and industrial work represent, indeed, the appropriate instrument of an education which is particularly concerned with the direct stimulation of the brain through the senses, and with the control of movement and ultimately, of self-control generally.
> (*Report of the Royal Commission on the Care and Control of the Feeble-Minded*, 1908, vol. 8, p. 108)

The aims of social control were thus seen to be directly realised via training for manual work.

This emphasis on vocational preparation for manual work as a major aim of special schooling, whether it was day or residential, was articulated more clearly during the 1920s, although the setting up of 'industrial colonies', segregating defective people, was never developed on any scale (Pritchard, 1963, chapter 14). However, this idea is by no means outmoded. An article by Jackson (1978) suggested that if the handicapped could not find employment on the open market, 'village communities' for the handicapped could be set up, in which they could live and 'work'.

The Wood Committee in 1929 wrote that:

It is obvious and universally admitted that the curriculum of
these [special] classes should devote less time than the
ordinary school to reading, writing and arithmetic and more
time to practical subjects such as bear directly on the child's
future, either in the home or in industry. (Wood Report,
1929, II, p. 151)

The committee stressed again that the major aims of special
schooling should be social adaptation and conformity, and the
ability to earn a living. This aim of creating self-sufficiency in
productive employment, while stressing desirable social qualities
needed to get and keep that employment, has persisted in special
education. An emphasis has always been placed on helping the
mildly handicapped, at least, to undertake productive work. As
Collman's (1956) study of the employment success of the ESN
noted: 'At least 70% of ESN ex-pupils are employable and this
group is a reliable source of labour.'

Special schools after the war, particularly for the ESN-M, have
embraced the aim of preparing their pupils for routine, manual
work with an emphasis on such qualities as obedience, docility
and punctuality. Knight and Walker (1965) discussed how the
school day could be made to approximate as closely as possible to
the factory day, and describe how in their schools pupils 'clocked-
in' at the wood-work room where 'one day a week we try to bring
factory-type conditions'. In a recent paper describing the work of
a Further Education College Industrial Training unit for slow
learners, Atkinson (1981) noted that while officially the aims of
the unit were to provide young people with occupational skills,
the day-to-day training is couched in terms of the model of a
'good worker' and the value of good work to those who control
the productive processes in society. As he noted, 'appearance,
demeanour, a willingness to accept subordinate roles and discipline, have a great influence on unit staff, and may be influential in
obtaining jobs for the students' (Atkinson, 1981).

The majority of special school leavers, then, have always followed a curriculum which had a general aim of preparing them
for some kind of low status employment. Indeed, in a dual-labour
market situation[5] where low-paid, manual, unsocial and insecure
jobs are undertaken by particular groups, the mildly handicap-

ped special school leaver has been able to move into these kinds of jobs. A report from one local education authority careers sub-committee in 1977 noted that:

> the majority of school leavers from special schools in 1974 found employment with comparative ease. The largest group of leavers were those from schools for the slow learners, and most had jobs as soon as term ended. They entered a variety of occupations – polishing, assembling, machine work, warehouse work, building, painting, polishing, canteen and occasionally office work.

However, the committee pointed to the effect of the employment situation in the 1970s as 'by 1975 many special school leavers were affected by the recession and those requiring routine or semi-skilled work found the most difficulty' (City of Birmingham, 1977).

The employment possibilities for special school leavers will be taken up later in this chapter and in the last chapter. Here it is important to note that the curriculum in special schools, particularly for the majority of handicapped children, those in the ESN-M schools and classes, has always, at least up to the present, had an overall aim of work-preparation which has taken precedence over basic literacy. It can be stressed again here that the curriculum decision has been implicitly taken to deny a large amount of 'knowledge', thought worthwhile and useful in normal schools, to future productive citizens, on the grounds that they are 'slow learners'.

There is, of course, a difference in the curriculum aims for the majority of children in special education, those in the non-normative categories, and the minority, those in the normative categories, where there is some general agreement that the children will rarely be productive or self-sufficient and may require some form of permanent care (see, for example, Brindley, 1979). Here a crucial, and historical, question is one of resources – how much money is the society willing to put into the education of children who will not provide any productive returns even via sheltered workshop employment? Nevertheless, a major curriculum aim for these children is still social control, expressed in terms of self-sufficiency if possible, social acceptance, and behaviour regulated by those who 'teach' the child.

It is in teaching these children that theoretical considerations of aims are most subordinated to practical considerations of classroom activity, as 'Aims may not directly suggest specific teaching needs' (Presland and Roberts, 1980, p. 29). The numbers of handbooks (Jefree *et al.*, 1977) and charts for assessing 'progress' for the severely subnormal (Gunzberg, 1977) testify to the need on the part of teachers to be told 'how' rather than 'why', and much of the 'how' involves control and direction of *all* the behaviour exhibited by the children. For example, Jefree's book includes a section on 'Dealing with inappropriate behaviour' (Jefree *et al.*, 1977, p. 90). It is here that the whole area of behavioural approaches in special education can be called into question. Given the unequal power relations between teachers, who define not only aims, but also 'appropriate behaviour', and can offer reward or punishment, and the pupils, whose intellectual, social and physical behaviour they are attempting to modify or change, it should be very important that teachers should be able to clarify and account for their practices.

Control and accountability

Questions concerning the control of the curriculum and accountability for curricular decisions have seldom been raised as far as special education is concerned. The development of the special school curriculum as 'practitioners talking to each other' was undoubtedly a result of the autonomy that heads and teachers in special schools have always possessed – a greater autonomy even than that engaged by their colleagues in normal schools. As Lawton has noted, 'Teachers in any system effectively have a good deal of control over the curriculum in the sense of what actually gets taught and how it gets taught' (Lawton, 1979, p. 10). But in special education teacher control has probably been carried to its furthest extreme.

The autonomy of special schools stems from the way in which they were allowed, from the outset, to make their own curriculum decisions, at a time when central control by the Education Department through its inspectorate was highly developed in normal elementary schools. From the outset there was to be no externally imposed curriculum. The London School Board, opening its first schools for special instruction in 1892, wrote to the Department of Education that 'the Board does not deem it desirable that they should be under an obligation to follow any definite curriculum for these special schools' (Pritchard, 1963, p. 121). The Wood Committee, in 1929, were enthusiastic about the way special schools had been allowed to develop internally. They 'possessed the advantage of freedom to adopt means to the required ends' (Wood Report, 1929, p. 55) — the ends, as the committee noted, being vocational preparation and 'self-respect and social control'.

After 1944 no curriculum content (apart from religious instruction) was specified for any, including special, schools. The subsequent Ministry of Education pamphlet, *Special Educational Treatment* (1946), specified 'treatment' in terms of type of school, methods and resources rather than curriculum content. For example, deaf children were to have 'hearing aids and courses in lip-reading where these are recommended by the School Medical Officer' (1946, p. 15), delicate children should have 'rest which takes place in the open-air after the mid-day meal' (1946, p. 16).

In the study undertaken by Tomlinson (1981) it emerged very clearly that head teachers of ESN-M schools, at least, had considerable discretion to decide on curriculum, pedagogy, organisation and 'ethos' in their schools. They also appeared to be much more idiosyncratic in shaping 'their' schools in accordance with their own personal styles than would be acceptable in normal schools. Thus, one head who believed in creating a 'therapeutic community' said that 'we are not after academic attainment, we see too many examples of the folly of developing specific skills out of context.' While another head, one of the few in the study who believed 'basic literacy' to be a goal for his school, said that 'urban children must be able to read and write — most of the children I get have enough between the ears to realise this.' Both heads apparently had the power to shape the curriculum in their schools according to these beliefs, with some negotiation with other teachers.

The heads did not feel they were as accountable to the local education authority or to parents over matters of curriculum and discipline, as heads of normal schools, and there was a noticeable lack of deference for the local education authority personnel. The local authority special schools administration had indeed seemed more willing at this time (1976) to leave the heads to 'get on with the job' and trust more to their experience and expertise than might be the case in normal schools.

In normal education there always has been 'curriculum control' by others, for example parents, employers, the local community, and external examinations, as well as local and central education authorities who have in the past provided and will provide increasingly in the future an influence on the curriculum (see, for example, Auld Report, 1979; Department of Education and Science, 1977a; Department of Education and Science Circular 14/77). Until very recently, special school teachers had to some extent been freer of these kinds of external control. In particular, special schools have always been free of the external influence of examination boards.

There are four possible reasons why control of the special school curriculum has been the prerogative of the heads and teachers, with fewer pressures for accountability from local or central education authorities, parents or employers. First, the clients of special education have already demonstrated that they cannot achieve the 'aims' their normal schools might have; they have already been assessed as deficient in terms of any normal educational goals. The major pressures on normal schools, to make children literate and provide an examination-credential oriented curriculum, 'goals' which have brought greater pressure for the accountability of teachers (Lawton, 1979, ch. 4), have not been seen as applicable to special schools. The goals of the special school curriculum are 'non-goals' in that there is no pressure to prepare children for examinations, to make them literate, or even, despite lip-service paid to the idea, to move children back into normal schools or classes. Second, the kind of pressures concerning educational standards and school preparation for employment (see Kogan, 1978 and Lawton, 1979, p. 39) have so far by-passed special education. With no public pressure concerning exams or standards, the need for accountability concerning the special school curriculum has largely been removed from practitioners. The kinds of 'curriculum control' envisaged by Reynolds in his initial definition of the term as 'the process by which decisions about the curriculum made within the school or the teaching profession are limited by outside interests – those of parents, employers, the local community or society at large' (Reynolds, 1982) are probably somewhat less applicable in special education than in any other form of education.

A third possible reason for the greater control and decreased accountability in special education has been the development of a powerful special education pressure group, comprising a variety of professionals and practitioners in special education who manage to define special education in their own terms and as their business and deflect too much outside scrutiny.[6] The section on parents (see chapter 5) has demonstrated the relative powerlessness of the clientele of special education – parents and children – and the ideologies generated by those in special education have often mystified critics. An example of this is the missionary ideology noted by Lindsey (1957), in which special school teachers were seen as undertaking unpleasant and perhaps dangerous work.

A fourth possible reason for greater autonomy in special schools may be the greater discretionary space[7] allowed to special schools to develop more personal relationships with pupils than is usually the case in ordinary state schools.

However, there are signs now that the debate on control and accountability in the rest of the education system may be reaching special schools. Lawton (1979) has discussed how the partnership model of control between central government and schools may now be changing to a more complex system of accountability as the DES seeks to gain a more general control over the school curriculum. He considered that this extension of central control may be taking place more by stealth than by open discussion, but in 1977 the DES invited LEAs to consult on a framework for the curriculum, particularly in relation to discussing common aims and a core curriculum (Department of Education and Science, 1977a, pp. 12–13). The consultation took the form of a circular in which a series of questions was posed to LEAs – one question concerned special education (Department of Education and Science, 1977a). When the replies had been collated, the DES produced another document which set out central government views on the form that a framework for the curriculum might take, bearing in mind the LEA response. Parts of this document are applicable to special schools – Section 12 specifically notes that 'special consideration shall be given by both local authorities and schools to the curriculum needs of ethnic minorities, the handicapped, the less able' and Section 18 notes that: 'in the course of public and professional debate about the school curriculum a good deal of support has been found for the idea of identifying a core or essential part of the curriculum to be followed by all pupils according to their ability' (Department of Education and Science, 1980a).

The document, *A Framework for the School Curriculum* (1980), has currently been offered to LEAs, heads and governors of special schools for comment. There is, it would seem, a greater demand for accountability concerning the special school curriculum and for the aims of special education to be clarified and for more open discussion to take place. However, given the confusion which exists over the curricular needs of the handicapped and the arguments over whether similar aims can be produced for differential ability, it is probable that central government intervention into the special school class or unit curriculum is less likely than intervention in the normal school curriculum. Heads and teachers in special education may continue to retain more power and autonomy than their colleagues.

The curriculum for slow learners

The extension of special education during the 1980s will focus attention much more sharply on the curriculum for 'slow learners', as these former ESN-M children from special schools and remedial children in normal schools will form the majority of 'unrecorded' children. Indeed, the majority of children in special education at the present and in the future will be the 'slow learners'. Brennan's (1979) project described them as 'the least academically successful 15–20% of the school population' (Brennan, 1979, p. 7).

A study of the history of special education during the twentieth century demonstrates the way in which links have come to be made between the children of manual working-class parentage and their 'slow learning' attributes (see chapters 2 and 3) which entail them being offered special educational treatment in the form of an inferior curriculum. It can be stressed again here that this kind of supposedly educational classification is not a 'neutral, helping Act' (Apple, 1979). There is, as Apple has pointed out, 'evidence that the label slow-learner, is massively applied to the children of the poor and ethnic minorities – much more so than the children of the economically advantaged and politically powerful' (Apple, 1979, p. 137).

The ideology of cultural disadvantage, and the humanitarian rhetoric of catering for needs, are currently so dominant in the thinking of practitioners that they largely take it as common-sense that slow-learning children will be of working-class origins, with a variety of accumulated deficits associated with the family environment (Gulliford, 1969, 1971). The 1980 conference of the National Council for Special Education was told that 'the most severely deprived disadvantaged children [are] much more worthy of special educational intervention than children of physical and mental handicap who are less economically stressed' (National Council for Special Education, 1980, p. 42). There is little evidence of a consideration of the curriculum for slow learners in terms of what it means to *withhold* knowledge from certain groups of children. As Brennan pointed out:

> If the transmission of some degree of common culture
> through a common curriculum is one purpose of education,
> at what point does the differentiated curriculum for the slow
> learner depart from that purpose? By what right is any child
> deprived of access to any corpus of human knowledge?
> (Brennan, 1979, p. 32)

Brennan's project did not study the social background of the slow-learning children in his sample as the *schools* in the sample provided information that their pupils mainly lived in older working-class houses or council houses, 60 per cent of the homes were lacking in intellectual stimulus, 50 per cent lacked regular routines, 23 per cent were affected by poverty, 18 per cent by illness or disability, 13 per cent were single-parent families and immigrant pupils formed 20 per cent of slow-learning pupils in the primary school studied (Brennan, 1979, p. 16).

These kinds of school observations are similar to those made to Dr Lewis in the 1920s for his report to the (1929) Wood Committee. The 'social problem class' of the 1920s and 1930s has become the culturally disadvantaged class of the 1970s and 1980s. The extensions of the attributes of slow learning and academic failure to a *larger* proportion of working-class children is coming at a time when, numerically and proportionally, manual workers form a smaller proportion of the socio-economic classes in Britain.[8]

The label 'slow learner', as Apple has pointed out (1979, p. 134), not only confers an inferior educational status but also an inferior social status, and disadvantage, as Rex and Tomlinson (1979, p. 168) have noted, is actually considered to be an intractable problem. Further, we have already noted earlier in this chapter that to be labelled a slow learner, remedial, mildly ESN, or whatever, is to be placed in a particular position with regard to future employment possibilities – the least secure, low-status sector of the labour market if employment is actually a possibility. In addition, the acquisition of any economic or political power, or even at worst, basic citizenship rights, becomes more difficult for slow learners.

To become a slow learner, then, means being reproduced in a sector of the manual working-class population as of low status, semi- or unskilled, or potentially unemployable.

What exactly passes for a curriculum for slow learners, is still largely an unknown quantity, and it is here that the autonomy of heads and teachers is most evident. Brennan's study offered a good literature review in which he identified seven approaches to slow learners which have been advocated, although there is little information as to which schools have adopted which approaches. The approaches range through curricula for what are currently known as severely subnormal to mildly subnormal or remedial. Thus, the approaches of *sensory training*, the *education of special groups* and *core programmes* refer to more severe 'learning problems', *watered-down curricula, concrete use of basic subjects, broad subject fields*, refer more to milder 'learning problems' and *units of experience* would refer to all groups (see Brennan, 1979, p. 30).

Referring to his 502 project schools, Brennan was able to write that:

> There was no evidence in the project schools that any LEA had developed any consistent attitude or policy about the detail of curricula in its schools, and no evidence of any agreed or centralised procedure for recording curricula. . . . This meant that the curriculum in each school is generated, developed and recorded within particular schools . . . one in

three primary schools, one in four secondary schools and one in six special schools did not supply any written accounts of curriculum. (Brennan, 1979, p. 62)

Thus, the LEAs did not have much information as to the curricula offered to slow learners in the schools; heads had powers to decide on the curriculum but even in schools with a written curriculum, 'what went on in classrooms often bore little relation to what should have been happening according to the documents' (Brennan, 1979, p. 63). Observation at two special (ESN-M) schools during 1975–6[9] indicated that heads and teachers do indeed have autonomy to shape the curricula of their schools, that the ultimate goal of schools with different methods and objectives was ultimately low-status employment and socially adjusted behaviour on the part of the pupils, although some schools are more successful at achieving these aims. Individual teachers, also, can operate independently to directives by heads or deputies.

The head of X school, like several schools I visited, said that this school took difficult children that other schools would not take. The school employed screening tests, developed by a doctor, to decide whether children were 'neurologically damaged' and other psychological tests to decide the level of intellectual functioning and ability. The head thought an IQ score was a good indicator of a child's potential. He said his school had a good reputation with local firms for sending boys who were good workers and 'able to get on with their mates and bosses'. He regarded this latter as a major aim of the school and all teachers were expected to stress social training. A document produced by the head read: 'Many special schools invariably fail by virtue of poor punctuality or attendance or inability to work in close proximity with others. The X school product has proved itself to be – on the whole – successful.'

The school is disciplined – children 'sit down and do as they are told', their day is structured and 'They know where they have to be and are punished if they are not there.' The school has 'Houses' and children gain points for good work and behaviour. In visiting individual classes, the first class teacher said she concentrated on making the children more acceptable to the general public, and on speech and communication. She thought very few of the children would learn to read and write. In the next class the teacher, who was taking an Open University degree, was more determined to teach literacy and had a structured programme of writing and perceptual training. In this school 'emotionally disturbed' children were grouped in a separate class and allowed a good deal of physical movement. At middle-school level a special class operates which aims to return children to normal school.

At Y school the head said that while he aimed to make his pupils work and society oriented, he placed more emphasis on an ethos of tolerance and acceptance in school and society. He had produced a document stating that the school was not after academic attainment . . . 'We want sensible use of language in real life, normal mannerisms, even if they are bad manners, easy relations with normal children born of independence, toughness and a socially acceptable appearance.'

The staff at this school carry keys. Windows, doors and cupboards are locked when not in use, and as the school has an ESN-S section, drugs are dispensed, mainly for quietening children. In the first class the teacher provided individual activities for the children and allowed a good deal of wandering and random behaviour. The second class was slightly more structured with matching, sorting and manipulating activities and some writing. In one middle-school class, creative activities and sport were stressed, the room was overflowing with boxes, dressing-up clothes and creative work done by the children, and each afternoon ended with football for the boys. The head of the secondary department disagreed with the head's curriculum ideas which he regarded as *laissez-faire*. He believed in a structured literacy programme with regular testing of children. Other teachers disagreed with this and discussions between staff occasionally became acrimonious. The school does not have as good an employment record as X school and the head was worried that this trend was growing during the recession.

The different ways in which some special schools go about preparing their pupils for self-sufficiency and low-status employment, if possible, may be one indication that while there may be some general agreement over this curriculum aim, there is little agreement over the method of achieving the aim. Curriculum aims for slow learners indicate the wider problem of 'what to do' with the handicapped in an industrial society. A further complexity for the schools comes when the rhetoric of 'help' is overtaken by economic reality and preparation of children for even the lower-status half of the dual-labour market becomes too expensive. Thus the Employment Rehabilitation Centres, set up in the early 1970s to prepare handicapped young people for work (Speake and Whelan, 1977), are now threatened with closure. This dilemma was succinctly posed in the columns of *The Times Educational Supplement*. 'If the Government really wishes to be seen to be taking the needs of handicapped young people seriously, it is worse than useless to be offering legislation with one hand and threatening to take away provision with the other' (*The Times Educational Supplement*, 8 August 1980).

The links between preparation for a job and the presumed social stability that this will engender, have always been important considerations in the special school curriculum. As the Warnock Report pointed out, it is in the interests of society to educate and train the handicapped. The group that has always been perceived as likely to be socially troublesome, the slow learner again, is especially singled out.

> A small amount of extra help for school leavers with
> moderate learning difficulties of emotional or behavioural
> disorders may enable them to hold down a job, and reduce
> the chances of them entering a cycle of frequent changes of
> job, leading to long-term unemployment and dependence on
> social or psychiatric services. (*Special Educational Needs* . . .,
> 1978, p. 163)

The overall curriculum aims of preparation for employment in low-status work and 'social adjustment' can be interpreted as indicating that special education may not be directed so much at catering for special needs and helping individual children as at providing a way in which potentially troublesome groups of children can be socially controlled. It is not surprising that upper- and middle-class parents do not subject their children to a curriculum for slow learners, despite Tredgold's assertion that upper-class dullards might be quite good at cabinet-making and poker work! (see chapter 3). The dominant social groups do not need their children to be controlled and directed into low-status employment.

Discussion of the special school curriculum is bound to be unsatisfactory at the present time. There are a variety of vested interests all attempting to provide the dominant context in which curriculum discussion should take place, for example, the War-nock approach, advocating a de-politicised philosophical context; psychologists advancing models of 'assessment and modification'; practitioners advancing a variety of curriculum objectives, content and methods and a confusion of the aims of special education for the non-normative groups with the normative groups. This chapter has attempted to provide some sociological input to the discussion by focusing on the curriculum offered to the majority of children in special education, the non-normative slow learners, and by suggesting that the special curriculum and its dissemination of 'non-knowledge' is related to economic, political and social structures of power and control.

The book now moves on to consider whether the treatment of a particular group of children, black children of former colonial origin, is also an indication of the power and control elements in special education.

The position of ethnic minority children in special education, particularly those of West Indian origin, is one of the clearest indications that this type of education does not exist solely to cater for the needs of individual children, but is related to the way particular groups are regarded as potentially troublesome to schools and society. Given the history of colonialism and white beliefs about the potential of black people (see Banton, 1979; Rex, 1971), it was highly probable that when black immigrant children began entering the education system in the early 1960s they would be regarded as a problem. Liberal pedagogic ideologies have always been stretched to their utmost in the assumption that black children were equal to white in most of the educative processes (Rex and Tomlinson, 1979, ch. 6). The general poor level of achievement of West Indian children in normal schools and their non-achievement through special schooling are not necessarily due to factors intrinsic to the children, but also to the ways in which the educational administrators and practitioners regard, and deal with, black children.

While this chapter concentrates on the issue of the over-placement of children of West Indian origin in the non-normative categories of special education, the treatment of ethnic minority groups can raise questions about the whole nature of special education. For example, if 'special needs' are difficult to define for indigenous children, and the causal factors behind these needs are unconsidered, how can professionals and practitioners claim to understand the special needs of minority group children? If the curriculum and its aims is unclarified for indigenous children, how can special schools adequately deal with minority children, particularly at a time when a multi-cultural curriculum is under consideration in education as a whole (Jeffcoate, 1979; James, 1979; Department of Education and Science, 1980a)?

Those who work in special education are often unaware of the connotations that the phrase 'special education' has taken on for some minority group parents in Britain. The number of West Indian children referred, assessed, and placed in schools for the mildly educationally subnormal has, for a number of years, been a particular emotive issue for the West Indian community in that it became symbolic of the general under-achievement of their children within the English school system (Tomlinson, 1978) and contributed to anxieties among first-generation immigrants that their children may be destined, through educational failure, to inferior employment and status. Towards the end of the 1970s, there has been similar anxiety about the numbers of West Indian children referred and placed in disruptive units and classes (Francis, 1979). Official anxiety over the general educational performance of children of West Indian origin contributed to the setting up of the Rampton Committee[1] in 1979, and the assessment of Performance Unit at the DES is considering a national survey on the issue (*The Times*, 30 December 1980c).

The legislative changes which will bring remedial and disruptive children officially into special education even though largely as non-recorded children will have a profound effect on the education of children of West Indian origin in Britain – the symbolic significance of the ESN issue will certainly become redundant as special education would become a major form of education for this particular minority group. In the context of the equal and just provision of education for the children of ethnic minority groups this would seem to be an unacceptable facet of multi-ethnic education. Many West Indian parents have never accepted the rhetoric that their children have special needs, and have become one of the first sustained pressure groups to protest about this kind of classification. Their protests may well be followed by other social groups as the results of expanded special educational treatment become apparent in the form of rejection by the labour market.

The problem of numbers

The current symbolic significance of the over-placement of children of West Indian origin in special (ESN-M) education can be better appreciated if the numbers in question are set against the total numbers of all children and the probable numbers of children of West Indian origin in maintained primary and secondary education. Table 7.1 demonstrates that in 1972, when the total school population in England and Wales was around nine million, 4,397 children of West Indian origin and 1,101 children of Asian origin were officially in all types of special education. As collection of statistics on immigrant children was discontinued in 1972, calculating numbers of percentage has become problematic since then. However, the 1972 figures showed that two-thirds of all 'immigrant' children in special education were of West Indian origin. Also in that year, although West Indian children as a whole constituted 1.1 per cent of all children in state schools, they constituted 4.9 per cent of all children in ESN-M schools (Tomlinson, 1978). The over-placement of West Indian children in ESN-M schools is demonstrated in Table 7.2. In 1972, at a time when the total percentage of children in ESN-M schools constituted less than 1 per cent (0.6 per cent in fact), the figure for West Indian children was almost 3 per cent.

Although there was a general decrease in referral and placement of all children in ESN-M schools in the mid-1970s, estimates indicated that West Indian children continued to be over-placed in proportion to their total numbers in the schools population. There is thus no question that children of West Indian origin have been over-referred and placed in this form of special education, which, as we have already noted, offers a non-credentialling, stigmatised form of education with much-reduced job prospects even for indigenous children.

Similarly, although numerical evidence is hard to acquire since collection of education statistics by ethnic origin ceased, it seems likely that children of West Indian origin are over-represented in the expanding existing statutory category of maladjustment, and in the numbers of disruptive centres and units – the 'multitude of sin bins' (Berger and Mitchell, 1978) which have developed on an *ad hoc* basis during the 1970s. An HMI survey, *Behavioural Units* (Department of Education and Science, 1978), found that 69 local

Table 7.1   New Commonwealth immigrant *a* children by category of special school, January 1972

		India	Pakistan	West Indies
Blind, partially sighted	B	26	16	44
	G	8	10	41
Deaf, partially hearing	B	44	27	172
	G	20	27	149
Physically handicapped	B	31	41	47
	G	24	12	41
Delicate	B	16	14	108
	G	15	6	54
Delicate and physically handicapped	B	21	17	44
	G	13	11	23
Maladjusted	B	4	2	202
	G	2	–	32
Educationally subnormal (M and S)	B	211	157	2,074
	G	187	75	1,248
Others (schools for epileptics, speech defects, etc.)	B	7	1	17
	G	2	2	2
Hospital schools	B	16	15	60
	G	8	10	38
Total	B	379	290	2,769
	G	279	153	1,628
		658	443	4,397
			1,101	
As a percentage of all immigrants in special schools	B	9.2	7.1	67.3
	G	11.0	6.0	64.0
As a total percentage of all immigrants in special schools		9.9	6.7	66.1

Source: DES *Statistics in Education – Schools*, 1972.
B= boys, G= girls

a Immigrant children were defined at this time as those born abroad or whose parents had lived less than ten years in Britain.

education authorities were operating a total of 239 units for nearly 4,000 pupils. An ACE survey (Advisory Centre for Education, 1980) found that 63 local education authorities were offering 5,857 places in 386 units – an increase of 48 per cent and 62 per cent respectively in two years. As Lloyd-Smith commented in an article in 1978:

> We have a new form of special provision, a new category of pupil and a new group of specialist teachers, . . . units may have the appearance of a neat remedy, but they have been adopted without sufficient consideration of the nature and meaning of disruptive behaviour. (Lloyd-Smith, 1978)

This is particularly relevant for children of West Indian origin in Britain. They live in a society in which white racism has become more and more respectable (Husbands, 1974; Rex and Tomlinson, 1979) and come from a culture which has been systematically down-graded. There are a variety of new forms of black consciousness development among the young, the cult of Rastafarianism being one of the most important (Cashmore, 1979). However, the overt political overtones of West Indian assertiveness are currently creating much anxiety in urban schools; any disruption of normal classroom activity by West Indian children

Table 7.2 All children, and West Indian children, in ESN-M schools and classes

Total number of children in maintained primary and secondary schools and in ESN-M schools and classes

	(1) Ordinary school	(2) ESN-M school	(3) (2) as a % of (1)
1972	9,032,999	60,045	0.66
1976	9,669,000	53,772	0.55

Total number of West Indian children in maintained primary and secondary schools and in ESN-M schools and classes

	(1) Ordinary school	(2) ESN-M school	(3) (2) as a % of (1)
1972	101,898	2,972	2.9
1976	125,000[a]	3,000[a]	2.4[a]

[a] Estimates assuming an increase in total school population and a decrease in ESN-M school population similar to indigenous children.

is regarded as a serious control problem by teachers (Tomlinson, 1981) and it is not particularly surprising that they should have become candidates for referral into 'disruptive' units. However, as Francis has pointed out:

> In the forefront of the sin-bin controversy has been the fear of black parents that the units could be turned into dumping-grounds, mirroring the ESN school battle of the 1960s. Units are one of the items under investigation by the Commission for Racial Equality in Birmingham and London. Many local community relations councils have expressed disquiet. (Francis, 1979)

The West Indian grievance

The West Indian community can be regarded as the first pressure group to sustain a protest and demand more clarity over the criteria used to decide on ESN-M placement. The North London West Indian Association expressed concern as early as 1965 that a disproportionate number of West Indian children was being placed in this form of special education. In 1967 an ILEA report noted that 28.4 per cent of children in ESN schools were 'immigrant', mainly of West Indian origin, and that in a survey of special schools the schools felt that a misplacement of these children was four times more likely due to methods and processes of assessment (Inner London Education Authority, 1968). In 1970 the North London West Indian Association lodged a complaint of racial discrimination against Haringey LEA, and although the Race Relations Board found no evidence of an unlawful act, they suggested that IQ tests might be unsuitable for the assessment of black children. It was interesting that in America in the same year the over-representation of black children in a similar type of special education, classes for the Educably Mentally Retarded, was becoming a cause for black parental anxiety. In San Francisco, where some 28 per cent of the city schools contained black pupils, 66 per cent of children in classes for the EMR were black. A group of black children in the city sued the California State Department of Education, and eventually a ban was placed on the use of IQ tests for purposes of assessment for EMR classes (Cookson, 1978).

However, the complexity of the referral and assessment procedures in England has always made it problematic to point simply to the culture-bias of IQ tests as a 'cause' of the over-placement of black children in ESN-M education. Asian children, who would be similarly handicapped by IQ tests, are not placed in disproportionate numbers, in the non-normative categories of special education. Bernard Coard, who in 1971 published a polemical paper entitled *How the West Indian Child is Made Educationally Subnormal in the British School System*, suggested that low teacher expectations and stereotypes about black children could lead to their over-referral, and the low self-esteem that black children acquire in a white racist society might influence their school performance. A letter sent to Chief Education Officers by the DES in 1973 on 'the educational arrangements for immigrant children who may need special education' mentioned the use of dialect English as a possible cause of education difficulties, and also teachers who could not cope with the learning problems and disciplinary of West Indian children in normal schools (Department of Education and Science, 1973).

The ESN issue continued to be a cause for concern throughout the 1970s, voiced in the columns of the black press and in evidence to government select committees. Articles in the journal *Race Today* in 1974 and 1975 pointed out that the issue had become symptomatic of the general failure of the school system to incorporate children of West Indian origin, and criticised the variety of explanations offered for the poor educational performance of West Indian children, particularly those centring on innate explanations, or 'deprivation' hypotheses (Dhondy, 1974; *Race Today*, 1975).

The evidence to the Select Committee on Race Relations and Immigration for their 1972–3 Report took evidence from sixteen official bodies concerned with the over-placement of West Indian children in ESN-M schools. Evidence from the Caribbean educationalists and community workers claimed that:

> Many children are packed off to ESN-M schools on the basis of inadequate assessment procedures. Very little consultation between the parents and the authorities takes place. Many parents are given inaccurate information as to the nature and purpose of ESN schools. (Select Committee on Race Relations and Immigration, 1973, vol. 3)

Despite a recommendation in this report that an annual review of the placement of immigrant children in special schools should take place, no action was taken and nine official bodies gave evidence to the Select Committee for its 1976 Report, *The West Indian Community*, again complaining about ESN schools. A witness from the West Indian Standing Conference wrote that 'this was one of the very bitter areas' for West Indians, and the Select Committee wrote in its Report that 'It is clear that the West Indian Community is disturbed by the under-achievement of West Indian children at school, and continues to be seriously disturbed by the high proportion of West Indian children in ESN schools' (Select Committee on Race Relations, 1976, vol. 1).

Evidence from Brent West Indian Standing Committee to this Committee indicated that while the ESN issue was largely symbolic, the large numbers of children who were placed in low streams or remedial classes in normal schools – those who will now form a large number of non-recorded children in special education – also created anxiety.

> Do not go away with the impression that our major interest is with ESN schools. We are concerned about them, but we are concerned more with the point that the majority of youngsters who have been to the so-called normal schools came out having achieved as little on the academic side as the children who went to ESN schools. (Select Committee on Race Relations, 1976, vol. 3)

Explanations for the generally poorer educational performance of children of West Indian origin have merged with explanations for their over-placement in ESN-M schools. In a review of thirty-three studies of West Indian school performance Tomlinson, 1980) in which twenty-seven studies indicated a lower performance than whites, explanations ranged through migration stress, family difference and disorganisation, childminding, domestic responsibility, dialect interference, low self-esteem, disadvantage, culturally biased tests, low teacher expectations, unsuitable curricula, low socio-economic class and racial hostility. However, it does appear that, when challenged, the education system will defend itself by reverting to innate individualistic explanations stressing the pupils' deficiencies. Thus, for example, in the aftermath of the Bristol 'riots' (National

Union of Teachers (Avon), 1980) the chairman of Avon County Council announced that black children were 'less academically inclined' and 'could not acquit themselves in ways which were attractive to employers' (*The Times Educational Supplement*, 30 May 1980).

The West Indian Community has a legitimate 'grievance' concerning the education of their children and have certainly not agreed that the placement of numbers of black children in the non-normative categories of special education has been a response to the children's special needs. Rather, they feel that the education system has a 'need' to deal with the children in this manner.

Professionals and West Indian children

The arguments in chapter 3 demonstrated that the social and cultural beliefs of professionals have always been reflected in the decisions and judgments they make when assessing children for the non-normative categories of special education. In the study of referral and assessment of ESN-M children undertaken in the mid-1970s (Tomlinson, 1981) an attempt was made to demonstrate that professionals also made decisions based on beliefs about the racial characteristics of particular children. It attempted to collect some empirical evidence as to why schools tended to over-refer children of West Indian origin, and why other professionals concur with the schools' judgments. In the study described in chapter 4 it was noted that all the professional people who had made a decision about the forty children (eighteen of them of 'immigrant' parentage) passing into special education were interviewed and a series of accounts, shown on p. 97, were abstracted to describe and explain 'ESN-M' children.

The referring heads are the people who actually make the initial decision to institute the process of ascertainment for special education, although usually after consultation with teachers. It was noted that in terms of accounting for ESN-M children, heads overwhelmingly used functional and behavioural criteria. Figure 7.1 demonstrates the variety of replies that the heads gave, the percentage of replies being shown in histogram form.

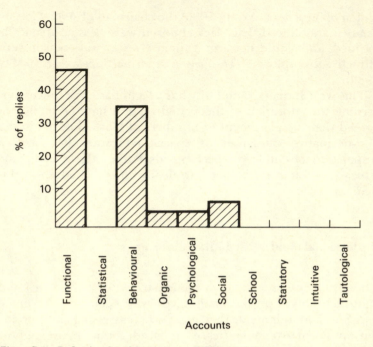

Figure 7.1   Referring heads' accounts of ESN-M children

Heads were also asked what they considered the educational problems of West Indian children to be. The result of this question is documented in Figure 7.2, and it is at once apparent that the criteria heads use to account for ESN-M children correspond almost exactly to their perceptions of the problem of West Indian children. The comments of the head teachers also indicated that they considered children of West Indian origin to possess 'natural' educational handicaps: the children were 'bound to be slower – it's their personalities', or they were described as 'a representative bunch, slow, docile and low-functioning', they were also 'less keen on education' than other children. Their behavioural problems were also taken to be a 'natural' characteristic, as one head said, 'They have the usual problems – hyperactivity and anti-authority.' All in all, the close correspondence between the heads' referral criteria for ESN-M education and their cultural perceptions of the 'natural' problems of West Indian children made it highly probable that West Indian chil-

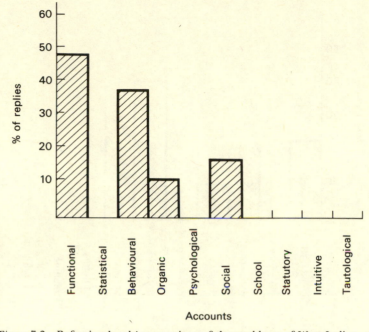

Figure 7.2   Referring heads' perceptions of the problems of West Indian children

dren would be regarded by heads of normal schools as likely candidates both for ESN-M education and, latterly, for 'special' education in behavioural units.

Once in the ascertainment process, 'immigrant' children appeared to be processed more speedily than indigenous children. The indigenous children in this study waited a mean of two years between referral and placement in special school; the immigrant children waited only eleven months. Decisions appeared to be made more speedily in the case of black children. Educational psychologists and medical officers, although more cautious than heads in attributing natural racial characteristics to West Indian children, did seem more likely to proceed with assessment on the basis of their beliefs. Psychologists, who, as noted in chapter 4, rejected accounts of ESN-M children as behaviour problems, did think that West Indian children were more likely to have behaviour problems and also social problems connected to 'disadvantage', as Figure 7.3 demonstrates.

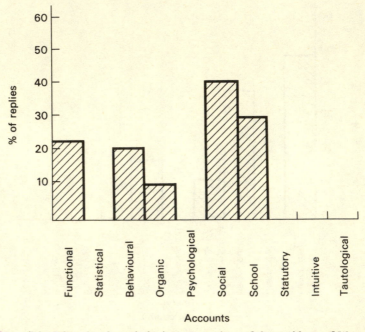

Figure 7.3   Educational psychologists' perceptions of the problems of West Indian children

Psychologists who relied on IQ test results, and believed that West Indian children had family problems and different developmental norms, were more likely to recommend ESN-M schooling. Those who were dubious about the value of IQ testing and the way in which normal schools went about educating West Indian children were less likely to recommend placement. However, one psychologist, who refused to test a West Indian boy on the grounds that the tests were culturally biased, did not, despite his liberal intentions, help the boy. The pupil, referred by his secondary school for low educational performance and bad behaviour, was sent to a guidance centre, then a suspension unit, and then, at sixteen, was allowed to leave the education system with no follow-up, and was soon in trouble with the police. Had he arrived in the ESN process he would have had a medical examination and the fact that he was deaf would presumably have been discovered (Tomlinson, 1981).

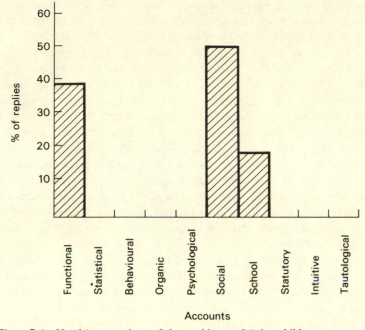

Figure 7.4 Heads' perceptions of the problems of Asian children

Medical officers, in common with other auxiliary professionals, also regarded West Indian children as potential behaviour problems. As one doctor said, 'They have ebullient natures, they can go berserk at school.' In general this study demonstrated that, despite the issue of their children being categorised out of normal education into special education causing acute anxiety to the black community, the professionals were not overtly informed or concerned. The actual referral and assessment procedures, based as they are on the cultural and racial beliefs of professionals, would certainly seem to work against the children of West Indian origin as far as the consideration of their 'special needs' is concerned.

Asian children in special education

The 'under-representation' of children of Asian origin in ESN-M education and in disruptive units has caused some comment among professionals and practitioners[2] although there are some indication that they are increasingly, in particular parts of the country, being put forward as candidates for the normative categories of special education, particularly deaf, partially sighted, physically and severely mentally handicapped. In Bradford in 1980 Asian children constituted 19.4 per cent of the general school population, but took 31 per cent of places in deaf schools and 22 per cent of places in schools for the partially sighted. Asian children in Britain reportedly have a higher death rate from congenital abnormalities – 8.7 per thousand, compared to 3.4 per thousand among the indigenous population. Explanations put forward to explain this include poor nutrition of mothers, larger families, reluctance to abort any abnormal foetus and recessive genes due to cousin intermarriage (*The Times*, 12 August 1980a).

However, in 1972 0.5 per cent of Indian and Pakistani children were in ESN-M schools compared to 0.6 per cent of the indigenous population and 2.9 per cent of West Indian children. Explanations for their under-referral into this type of special education would seem to centre on the professionals' perceptions of the school problems of Asian children. As shown in Figure 7.4, Asians do not meet the head teachers' criteria for referral into ESN-M education. Their functional problems were considered to be related to language, but they were not considered to have any 'natural' or intransigent educational or behavioural problems. Asian children are regarded as 'keen on education' and their parents are perceived as valuing the educative process. Heads stressed what they perceived as the social deficiencies of Asian families, cultural and language problems, but these do not constitute referral criteria into special education. Similarly, Asian children are not, as a group, perceived as a threat to the normal order of schools by 'bad' or disruptive behaviour and there has, so far, been no evidence that numbers of Asian children are placed in behavioural units.

It does not seem likely that Asian children will be particularly affected as a group by new legislation in special education. Although special educational needs are equated with 'learning difficulty' in the 1981 Education Bill, and language problems might be thought to lead to 'learning difficulty', the Bill specifically lays down that 'a child is not to be taken as having a learning difficulty solely because the language (or form of language) in which he is taught is different from a language (or form of language) which at any time has been spoken in his home' (Education Bill 1981, clauses 1–4).

West Indian children and new legislation

The recommendation of the Warnock Committee and the embodiment of some of these recommendations in proposed new legislation (Department of Education and Science, 1980b, Education Bill 1981) will have far-reaching consequences for a large number of children of West Indian origin in schools. The Warnock Report touched on the issue of the disproportionate number of West Indian children in ESN-M schools in one paragraph, out of 416 pages (*Special Educational Needs* . . ., 1978, p. 64) and noted that 'any tendency for educational difficulties to be assessed without proper reference to a child's cultural and ethnic background and its effect on his education can result in a category of handicap becoming correlated with a particular group in society', and that the 'uncertain relationship between remedial and special education' might prove to be a problem for certain ethnic groups. However, the paragraph went on optimistically to comment that no variation in assessment procedures should be envisaged for ethnic minority children as, providing cultural factors were taken into consideration, parents would come to view assessment 'not with suspicion, but as offering the possibility of enhanced educational opportunity for their children' (p. 64).

In the light of evidence over the past fifteen years it seems unlikely that the West Indian community will view any form of special education for their children as enhanced educational opportunity. The Warnock Report recommended:

1 that a meaningful distinction between remedial and special education can no longer be maintained and that former remedial children should be described as children with learning difficulties;
2 that special education embraces educational help for children with emotional and behavioural disorders who have previously been regarded as disruptive.

If children of West Indian origin continue to be over-represented in the non-normative categories of special education, it would seem that around one-third or more of all West Indian children in schools would in the future be candidates for some form of special educational provision.

The basis for calculation of these numerical possibilities must lie in the examination of the current referral and assessment criteria for the non-normative categories of special education, in the current placement in remedial classes of a number of West Indian children in schools, and in the schools' perception of disruptive behaviour. To recapitulate on these: the stereotyped beliefs which professionals, and practitioners, particularly teachers, hold about West Indian children's ability, behaviour and attitudes to education, together with an acceptance that these are somehow 'natural' racial attributes, have in the past made it likely that West Indian children would meet the criteria for referral into the non-normative areas of special education. The assumption that black children start 'equal' in the referral and assessment processes, with no account being taken of the fact that these children are being educated in a largely hostile white society, in which even professionals are influenced by post-colonial beliefs, have further 'disadvantaged' West Indian children in the processes leading into special education. There is no reason to suppose that under new legislation, beliefs and assumptions made by professionals will be changed. Indeed, teachers, who hold the most stereotyped beliefs about black children (Brittan, 1976; Giles, 1977; *Cause for Concern*, 1978; Edwards, 1979), will be the people who will initiate and participate in the first three stages of decision-making as to whether children have special educational needs. It also seems likely that similar beliefs and assumptions, which have influenced over-referral into ESN-M education, have also influenced the categorisation of numbers of West Indian children as remedial. Teachers have tended to regard the learning problems of West Indian children as somehow 'natural' and intransigent, and have had lower expectations of good academic performance. There is no reason to suppose that the numbers of 'remedial' West Indian children in schools will diminish. The inclusion of disruptive units and centres in new legislation as answering special educational needs certainly offers official recognition on what is already happening – these units are already looked on as a form of special education to which children can be referred more quickly than using the long-drawn-out old assessment procedures for the old statutory non-normative categories of ESN-M and maladjusted.

The terms of the white paper proposing new legislation, that it 'will include not only those difficulties which arise from physical or mental disability, but also those which may be due to some other cause' (Department of Education and Science, 1980b, p. 12), are ominous words when applied to West Indian children. There has been, and will be, considerable disagreement over the 'cause' of the poorer educational performance of West Indian children, and their disruptive behaviour in schools. Under new legislation, the exclusion of even larger numbers of these children from normal education and their placement in special education – even in 'non-recorded' special education – may mean that special education becomes a major form of education for children of West Indian origin.

While some writers have been concerned to demonstrate what one considered to be 'real purpose of British Schools – the maintenance of white supremacy' (Phillips, 1979) by the over-placement of black children in the stigmatised, non-normative parts of the education system to ensure their low socio-economic status, this chapter has been included to provide evidence that there are groups in the society who vehemently oppose the benevolent rhetoric that their children have 'special needs', and point instead to the 'needs' of a society that denies certain groups of children a normal education.

In the final chapter on the future of special education, the ways in which new legislation will assist in the movement into some form of special education of all groups who might be troublesome in normal education will be examined.

Chapter Eight · The future of special education

From the point of view of practitioners and professionals the future of special education currently appears very uncertain. The economic circumstances of the early 1980s and cuts in the overall education budget appear to threaten the existence, and certainly the expansion, of this sub-section of the education system. The president of the National Council for Special Education spoke in April 1980 of 'new-style Luddites who have won power and are wielding axes against all social machinery', including the machinery of special education (National Council for Special Education, 1980). Practitioners have, since the mid-1970s, demonstrated their anxiety that the integration movement might threaten their hard-won 'special' expertise, that normal schools will retain what special schools have come to regard as *their* rightful clients, and that the rationale for this special sub-section of the education system would disappear (see, for example, Ainscow *et al*., 1978; National Union of Teachers, 1979). The section included in the 1981 Education Bill, empowering local authorities to close special schools, may also cause some anxiety.

However, this short-term viewpoint may be unduly pessimistic. Without historical, comparative, and sociological perspectives, practitioners may not always be able to analyse clearly the nature and purpose of special education in late twentieth-century industrial societies and may therefore minimise its, and their own, importance. What is more likely to happen is that special education, in changed forms, and rationalised by changing ideologies, will continue to expand and become a *more* important part of the whole educational system.

A respected practitioner in special education recently described its growth as a 'historical accident' (Hoghugi, 1980). Now, one of the first points made in this book was that no part of any education system develops spontaneously or accidentally. The development of education systems and the forms that they take are the result of decisions on the part of individuals or groups with power, who control resources which they can give or withhold. The social, political, economic and professional vested interests which have dictated the growth and development of special education have not disappeared, and the control of decisions and money by individuals and groups remains.

A sociological analysis

It has been a purpose of this book to introduce Wright Mills's (1959) 'sociological imagination' into an analysis of special education and to try to relate processes in special education to the wider social structure, and it is contended here that it is only on this basis that adequate discussion of the future of special education can take place. As long as debates in special education continue to take place solely within the constricting context of individualistic psychologically-oriented appraisal[1] or in a supposedly a-political philosophical context[2] and as long as practice continues to be rationalised by the ideology of benevolent humanitarianism and the rhetoric of special needs, it will become more difficult for all concerned with special education to make sense of the processes and issues. What can the sociological imagination suggest is happening in special education, in terms of changes in form, purpose and ideologies? This book began by suggesting that state special education developed and took the forms it did to cater for children who had been categorised out of the normal education that was offered to the majority of children, and that its development had more to do with the 'needs' of an industrial society which was endeavouring to produce and train a stable, docile, productive workforce, than with the 'needs' of individual children. The smooth running of normal schools and, latterly, their examination-oriented, credentialling functions, were impeded by troublesome children who could not, or would not, conform to the requirements of schools, particularly in terms of learning capabilities and appropriate behaviour.

Humanitarian ideologies and Christian reformist principles were used to rationalise the removal of the defective, handicapped or those in 'need' into a special education sector which has expanded continuously. The expansion has substantially benefited a variety of professional groups. However, a number of conflicts and contradications have always been inherent in this dynamic process. First, the profit motive and work ethnic of industrial societies have dictated that as many of the handicapped be prepared for productive employment as possible, a demand which is rationalised by the idea that to work is to be 'normal'; but contradictions arise if the handicapped cannot or do not want to work, or if the kind of low-status employment for which they are primarily destined is disappearing.

Second, there have always been contradictions concerning the amount of money which the government considers should be spent on educating the handicapped or troublesome. The Lord Chancellor in 1893 was worried that 'too many' defective children would be discovered by local authorities (Pritchard, 1963, p. 149) and the government currently plans 'a reduced total level of public expenditure on education' which will affect special education by 1983 (Department of Education and Science, 1980b, p. 9). It will certainly be cheaper to educate children with special needs in ordinary rather than special schools.

Third, the majority of children categorised out of normal state education into the non-normative categories of special education have always been working-class children, particularly male children, who have been most troublesome to schools in terms of their 'slow learning' capacities or disruptive behaviour. There has always been a contradiction to be resolved in presenting these children as handicapped or in special need, *on the same terms* as children with normative handicaps or needs. It was suggested in chapter 3 that one way in which this has been resolved is by adding the ideology of cultural disadvantage to that of benevolent humanitarianism and presenting special education as 'doing good' to working-class and, latterly, black children. Chapter 7 demonstrated that black parents in Britain have always challenged the ideology that their children have 'special needs' and have sustained pressure on the educational administration and protested about the categorisation of what they regard as too many black children into special education. They may very well be in the vanguard of protests from the white working class who will find more of their children in the future being offered a special, rather than a normal, education, even if this special education takes place within the ordinary school. This will certainly mean that new ideologies and rationalisations will have to be employed to persuade parents that their children need special education, although, as the 'parents' section in chapter 5 demonstrated, coercive measures have already been incorporated into legislation to be used if persuasion fails. Indeed, future legislation, in the form of the 1981 Education Bill, is as coercive towards parents as previous legislation.

The new tripartite system

To understand the changing forms and ideologies in special education, it is necessary to understand developments and changes in the whole education system, particularly changes since the virtual establishment of a state comprehensive system of secondary education during the 1970s. The old tripartite system – grammar, technical and secondary modern schooling – established after the 1944 Education Act, had become untenable by the 1960s. A common school underpinned by egalitarian ideologies, and attended by middle- and working-class children, was envisaged and supported by all social classes (Ford, 1969). The upper classes continued, as they had always done, to send their children into independent fee-paying education. Reynolds and Sullivan (1979) have argued that the 1970s, the period when comprehensive schools were developing, was a period when the state education system was left relatively free to develop curricula, pedagogies and forms of control with little outside interference. This argument is certainly substantiated by the increased use that the schools made of remedial classes, and by the development of behavioural units for disruptive pupils. Comprehensives attempted to solve the problem of incorporating larger numbers of troublesome working-class pupils by segregating them internally within the school. One reason for the expansion of special education to include remedial and disruptive children is that it provides legitimation for the methods the comprehensives had developed on an *ad hoc* basis to solve urgent problems of control. Reynolds and Sullivan believe that most comprehensive schools have moved towards the increased coercion of all but the most able children, and that this is having the effect of alienating more children, particularly those in the lower third of the ability range (Reynolds and Sullivan, 1979, p. 56). Thus there are likely to be more children in comprehensives who are troublesome to the school's organisation.

Reynolds has further argued (1981) that the comprehensive schools did not, during the 1970s, change the kind of 'knowledge' they were offering; they attempted to incorporate a subject-oriented grammar-type curriculum and were subject to increasing pressure from the middle class to maintain the characteristics of grammar schools in terms of academic goals, character-building, and preparation for higher-status occupations. Now, the pressures on comprehensives to produce 'grammer-type' pupils while at the same time incorporating more 'secondary-modern' type working-class children who would not, or could not, conform to the learning and behavioural expectations has been partially solved by the recommended expansion of special education. It is not accidental that the recommendations of the Warnock Report to expand special education to include the remedial and disruptive should come at a time when comprehensive schools, and even state primary schools, are seeking a rationalisation for the exclusion of larger numbers of troublesome children from normal classes. The state education system will only contrive to function efficiently and provide professional and semi-professional workers, skilled and service workers, if as many non-conformist and troublesome children as possible are categorised out of it into some form of special education. The wording of new legislation (1981 Education Bill) is sufficiently vague to allow for the removal of a wide variety of children into special education. Thus, a child will have special educational needs if he has a learning difficulty which calls for special educational provision. The learning difficulty can be diagnosed if:

> a) he has a significantly greater difficulty in learning than the majority of children of his age, or b) he suffers from a disability which either prevents or hinders him from making use of educational facilities of a kind generally provided in schools. (1981 Education Bill, clause 1)

But to categorise children out of normal education has overtones of the segregation of the handicapped, which current ideologies of egalitarianism oppose. Notions of egalitarianism will continue to be served by the movement towards integration. Ostensibly, as many children as possible will be taught in a common comprehensive school with their special needs catered for. Even children on whom the local authority will 'maintain a statement' are to be taught in ordinary school providing that this is compatible with:

> a) the child receiving the special educational provision he requires, b) the provision of efficient education for the children with whom he will be educated, and c) the efficient use of resources. (1981 Education Bill, clauses 2–3).

In practice, this will mean that larger numbers of mainly working-class and black children will be segregated in special units or classes and thus officially be placed in special education, albeit as non-recorded children on whom the LEA does not 'maintain a statement'. In terms of the normal goals of the school that they attend, they will be offered a 'non-education', which will fit them only for low-status employment or unemployment. Indeed, special education within normal schools may develop as a powerful legitimator for the increasing unemployment of a larger number of young people. To have received a special education – with its historical stigmatic connotations – even a non-recorded special education in an integrated setting, will be regarded unfavourably by potential employers. This may be as true for the normative categories of handicap as for the non-normative – the physically handicapped, blind, deaf, etc., may be prototype groups in society who are increasingly offered 'directed' or 'sheltered' work and lives.

While comprehensive schooling was developing during the 1970s, the independent sector of education was continuing to expand (Bridgeman and Fox, 1978). More middle-class parents, believing that comprehensives can no longer cater for their needs – which are to reproduce their children as middle-class people with good occupational positions – were opting out of state education and buying independent education.

It is contended here in this final chapter that a new tripartite system of education may be developing in Britain, comprising independent schooling, comprehensive schooling and special schooling. There will be some overlap between these sections as a large number of children with 'special needs' will be integrated and offered their special education within the comprehensive school,[3] and some children, particularly those in the normative categories such as the blind or deaf, who have always relied on independent provision, will continue to attend independent schools. Thus, a new tripartite system of education for all children may develop as follows:

Some overlap   independent education
                comprehensive education
                special education

Structural perspectives

The suggestion that special education may come to form part of a new-style tripartite system of education is one way of relating changes in forms and ideologies in special education to the wider social structure: as such it is a structural perspective. In chapter 1 it was suggested that from structural perspectives – particularly conflict perspectives informed by an historical dimension – it was possible to raise questions about the whole development and purpose of special education in industrial society. It is only by turning the rhetoric of the 'special needs of children' around, and asking what are the needs and interests of dominant groups in education and the wider society, who have influenced the development of special education, that a clearer analysis can be made. But this kind of analysis is dependent on the conflict theories which were briefly reviewed in chapter 1, and need to be noted again here.

Like the structural functional theorists in education (for example, Halsey *et al.*, 1961), conflict theorists (for example, Bowles and Gintis, 1977) argue that the goals and functions of all parts of the education systems in industrial societies are substantially determined and constrained by external social, political and economic factors and interests. Much of the discussion of aspects of special education in this book has been based on an acceptance of this argument. It was also suggested in chapter 1 that the theories of the French sociologists Bourdieu and Passeron (1977) might provide useful insight into understanding the role of special education in industrial societies. They argue that while schools appear to offer all pupils the means of succeeding in social and occupational hierarchies, they actually function to preserve the social, economic and cultural *status quo*. The society perpetuates and reproduces the conditions for its own existence by the transmission or withholding of varying amounts and kinds of education to different social groups. Ostensibly fair assessment procedures legitimate the categorisation of certain children out of normal education. Bourdieu and others have pointed to the way in which ideologies are used to rationalise these procedures. Apple, for example (1979, p. 164), has discussed the way in which a 'treatment' language on the part of educators – an example of which would be the assessment and treatment of special needs – can become an ideological justification for the social and behavioural control of certain children.

The expansion of special education to include even more children about whom there can be no normative agreement as to their 'special needs' could lead to a situation where special education becomes a more overt form of social control. Those who receive a special education will be subject to more direction and control, not only during the school process, but also after leaving school. To have special educational needs catered for may, in itself, become for some children a handicap for life.

The implementation of the new tripartite system of special education and the expansion of special education will require justification, and it is here that ideology becomes important. It is likely that the ideology of benevolent humanitarianism, which has always provided a justification for professional and government intervention and action in special education, will continue to operate. Within this ideology professionals can genuinely believe that they are 'doing good' and can minimise the extent of their own economic and professional vested interests. Governments will use the ideology to rationalise their extended influence, whether they are increasing or decreasing funding and resources. For example, the DES paper on special needs (1980b), after threatening a reduction in spending of special education, concludes with the assurance that 'the government believes that the proposals in this white paper will advance the cause of those of our children and young people for whom the community rightly has a special concern'. However, there are signs that this kind of

rhetoric may be challenged more explicitly in the future, particularly if a 'special' education is seen by parents to minimise rather
than maximise their children's life-chances and opportunities.

The 1980s will undoubtedly see the growth of more pressure
groups on behalf of the normative categories in special education
– those who may as children be described as having special needs,
but who will grow into adults described as 'disabled' or 'handicapped'. For example, a group of parents in Oxfordshire are currently pressing the DES and their LEA to fulfil their responsibilities under the 1944 Education Act, and provide adequate
further education for the handicapped (Newell, 1981). It is
doubtful whether pressure groups will develop to press the interests of the children in the non-normative categoriés, who, as this
book has continually stressed, are the majority of children in
special education. Children who are 'maladjusted' or who have
'mild learning difficulties' are more likely to be labelled as adults
with pejorative labels and will not attract interest and sympathy.

Structural approaches in education, as Squibb has noted
(1981), may be suggesting ideas and insights which are uncomfortable for teachers and other professionals trained in, and
committed to, a body of educational doctrine which emphasises
individualism and idealistic values. But it is only by moving from
individualistic to structural analysis that it becomes possible to ask
broader questions about the aims, forms, ideologies and changes
in special education. Asking, and attempting to answer, these
broader questions should certainly provide all those concerned
with special education with a clear understanding of the enterprise in which they are engaged, how change could affect them,
or how they can influence the direction of change.

The needs and interests of professionals

Professionals and practitioners in special education will have a
need in the future to understand the development and purposes
of special education, and their own roles in it, more clearly.
Future conflicts in special education may centre less on the kind
of rivalry between professional groups that has characterised the
history of special education and more on conflict with central and
local administration, who may increasingly attempt to influence

the direction of special education, particularly by giving or with-holding resources. It was suggested in chapter 1 that conflict perspectives are useful in explaining the way in which dominant group interests can shape the structures and processes of education and can illuminate the conflicts and tensions between the various groups involved in special education.

The history of special education can be viewed partly in terms of the benefits that medical, psychological, educational and other personnel derived from its development and expansion, and the needs and interests of these professionals will certainly be advanced by the proposed expansion of special education, as they have in the past. The new processes of referral and assessment will increase the numbers and types of professionals whose judgments are used in the assessment processes – medical, psychological and ancillary professionals beyond stage 3 of the new processes, and heads, teachers, advisors, special teachers and psychologists up to stage 3. Developing special education in integrated settings will demand more, not less, professional expertise, and the increased use of professional mystiques may be used to legitimate the processes that segregate normal from special. Indeed, if the ideology of benevolent humanitarianism needs supplementing, it may well be done by the increased use of professional judgments. As Larson (1977) noted, professional judgments can be used as forms of ideological control and may be used much more to persuade reluctant parents that their children have special needs. The 'needs' of more professionals will certainly be served by the expansion of special education into new forms.

Professional involvement in special education has always been marked by tension and conflicts of interests, as chapter 4 demonstrated. The historical antipathies and conflicts between medical, psychological and educational personnel, and between different practitioners in education, are still present, but there are signs that these antipathies may be played down as mutual interests are identified. If the needs of all professionals are reasonably satisfied as the revised and expanded system of special education is worked out, this part of the education system will be able to consolidate mutual professional autonomy.

However, it has already been suggested that in the future tensions may centre more on conflicts between professional autonomy and government administration. Professionals are increasingly being used as experts with rational knowledge by state bureaucracies, to legitimate administrative 'needs' and decisions, and to provide the ideological rationalisations for state action. Professionals who wish to retain and develop their own autonomy may resent being used as 'servants of the state' and object to their expertise being used to rationalise administrative decisions. Professionals may also find that they have to cope with the increase in 'client power', as parent groups and pressure groups become more developed and organised in special education, and may have to develop strategies to cope with this.

Conclusion

This book set out to widen debates in special education by introducing a variety of sociological perspectives and by suggesting that these could illuminate issues, policies and practices in special education. The particular perspective sustained in the book has been a structural-conflict perspective within which the interests of different groups concerned with special education, the power and resources they command, the beliefs, ideologies and rationalisations that they employ to legitimate their practices, and the way in which their practices affect the relatively powerless clients in special education, have been touched upon.

It has also been stressed that development and changes in special education cannot be fully understood without a historical understanding of the social origins of this important part of the education system. The overall aim of the book has been to introduce the 'sociological imagination' into an area dominated by medical, psychological and philosophical input, and to begin to suggest some ways in which sociological perspectives might inform debates and issues in special education. Special education must be understood as a social process, set within a social and political context if the special needs of children are to be truly served. These special needs may be construed as the private troubles that C. Wright Mills wrote of, but they are related to the public issues as to why a society decides to separate, however minimally, and in whatever way, children who are special from children who are normal.

Notes

1 Why a sociology of special education?

1 There is a large literature on the nature of the state and the relationship between the state and education. (See, for example, chapter 1 of *The State, the Family and Education* by Miriam David.) In this book the state is viewed as central government in Britain, with the Department of Education and Science being regarded as a government institution.

2 See, for example, M. M. Lindsey (1957). This point will be further discussed in chapter 4.

3 *The Times*, 12 July 1980: 'Blind given hope for artificial sight'.

4 For example, Tizard and Grad (1961); Sheridan (1965).

5 For example, Collman (1956) and Jerrold and Fox (1968).

2 The social origins of special education

1 See Archer (1979, ch. 2), for a discussion of the notion of 'dominant groups' in education.

4 Professional roles and the assessment process

1 Enforceable procedures are those built into the law via the Education Acts of 1914, 1921 and 1944 and no change in these procedures is envisaged in post-1981 legislation.

5 Parents, pupils and teachers in special education

1 Grammar schools for blind children were set up at Worcester in 1866 for boys, and Chorley Wood in 1924 for girls.

2 The cases of 'Jimmy' and 'Albert' were recorded during observations in ESN-M schools in 1976.

3 See *Special Education. Forward Trends*, vol. 1, no. 1, 1974 – 'A teacher's guide to drugs'.

4   The *Special Schools' Journal* was the journal of the Special Schools'
Association which in 1962 became the Association for Special
Education. In 1974 this association merged with the College of
Special Education and the Guild of Teachers for Backward Children,
to form the National Council for Special Education and published a
new journal, *Special Education – Forward Trends*, in March 1974.
5   These conflicts are not documented as little research has been
undertaken specifically examining the 'integration' of ESN-S
children and their teachers over the past decade.
6   The revised prospectuses of fifteen colleges and universities offering
courses in special education in 1980 were reviewed.

6   The curriculum in special schools

1   The Schools Council for Curriculum and Examinations was formed
in 1964. The council has sponsored five projects concerned with
special education out of 140 projects sponsored during the 1960s and
1970s and a working party on Special Education was set up in 1969.
The Warnock Committee recommended that a special section of the
Schools Council be set up to develop and disseminate curriculum
materials for special education.
2   John Reynolds made this point clear to me. He suggested that
alternative models for special schools curricula might be more
appropriate to the means-end model. He is also critical of the
'correspondence' view followed in this chapter that curriculum
control can be interpreted as social control.
3   The preoccupation with the means-end model is currently to be seen
in the development of technical aids, for example the use of
micro-computers in special schools. An article by Staples and Lane
(1980) noted that 'to use the computer efficiently in teaching, the
curriculum model proposed within Warnock must be followed'.
4   I am indebted to Michael Barrett for drawing my attention to the
'three Ms'.
5   For an explanation of dual-labour market theory see Doeringer and
Piore (1971). The low-status occupations tend to be taken by blacks,
immigrant groups, women and the handicapped.
6   There are large numbers of professional and voluntary organisations
(some documented by Segal, 1974; see also National Council for
Special Education, 1980); their influence on the curriculum in special
education is a subject as yet unresearched.
7   Acknowledgments to John Reynolds for this suggestion.
8   See Halsey, Heath and Ridge (1980). Only 22.6 per cent of the

working population can now be classed as semi- or unskilled manual workers in industry.
9   These observations are offered as descriptive case studies only. They are *not* part of any rigorous observational study of special schools.

7   Ethnic minority children in special education

1   A committee of inquiry into the education of Ethnic Minority Children, under the chairmanship of Anthony Rampton, was set up in 1979.
2   Private conversations with heads. One special (ESN-M) school head was of the opinion that Asian children were 'missing out' by not making use of this type of schooling.

8   The future of special education

1   Research and debate in special education continues to be dominated by psychologists, particularly those working at the prestigious institutes concerned with special education – the Hestor Adrian Centre in Manchester and the Thomas Coram Institute in London.
2   The a-political philosophical context advocated and practised by Mary Warnock was referred to in chapter 3. But philosophers themselves, particularly at Oxford University, are in a particular position in relation to social and political structures.
3   See chapter 3, p. 78, for a discussion of the types of intergration advocated by the Warnock Report. Children can be placed in units or centres away from the school, but, by remaining on the school roll, are still officially integrated.

Bibliography

ADVISORY COUNCIL FOR EDUCATION (1980), 'Survey of Disruptive Units', Mimeograph, London.

AINSCOW, M., BOND, J., GARDNER, J., and TWEDDLE, D. (1978), 'A new role for the special school', *Special Education — Forward Trends*, vol. 5, no. 1.

A New Partnership for our Schools — A Report of the Committee of Enquiry into the Management and Government of Schools (1977), HMSO, London (the Taylor Report).

APPLE, M. (1979), *Ideology and Curriculum*, Routledge & Kegan Paul, London.

ARCHER, M. S. (1979), *The Social Origins of Education Systems*, Sage, London.

ATKINSON, P. (1981), 'Labouring to learn. Industrial training for slow learners', in L. Barton and S. Tomlinson (eds), *Special Education — Policy, Practices and Social Issues*, Harper & Row, London.

ATTWOOD, A. J. (1977), 'The priority parents' workshop', *Child Care. Health and Development*, vol. 3.

AULD, R. (1979), *William Tyndale Junior and Infant School Public Enquiry*, Inner London Education Authority, London.

BALLANTYNE, J. (1977), *Deafness*, Churchill Livingstone (3rd edn), London.

BANDURA, A. (1977), *Social Learning Theory*, General Learning Press, New Jersey.

BANTON, M. (1979), *The Idea of Race*, Tavistock, London.

BARROW, R. (1978), *Radical Education*, Martin Robertson, London.

BARTLEY, G. C. T. (1871), *The Schools For the People*, Bell & Daldy, London.

BARTON, L., AND MOODY, S. (1981), 'The value of parents to ESN (S) school — an examination', in L. Barton and S. Tomlinson (eds), *Special Education — Policy, Practices and Social Issues*, Harper & Row, London.

BARTON, R. (1973), 'The institutionalized mind and the subnormal mind', in H. Gunzberg (ed.), *Advances in the Care of the Mentally Handicapped*, Baillière-Tindall, London.

BECKER, H. S. (1963), *Outsiders*, Free Press, New York.

BELL, P. (1970), *Basic Teaching for Slow Learners*, Muller, London.

BERGER, A., and MITCHELL, G. (1978), 'A multitude of sin bins', *The Times*

Educational Supplement, 7 July.

BERGER, P. and LUCKMANN, T. (1971), *The Social Construction of Reality*, Penguin, Harmondsworth.

BERNSTEIN, B. (1970), 'Education cannot compensate for society', *New Society*, 26 February.

BERNSTEIN, B. (1971), *Class, Codes and Control*, vol. 1, ch. 10, 'A Critique of the Concept of Compensatory Education', Routledge & Kegan Paul, London.

BERNSTEIN, B. (1975), *Class, Codes and Control*, vol. 3, Routledge & Kegan Paul, London.

BINET, A., and SIMON, T. (1914), *Mentally Defective Children* (trans. W. R. Drummond), E. J. Arnold, London.

BOOTH, T. (1978), 'From normal baby to handicapped child', *Sociology*, vol. 12, no. 2.

BOSWELL, D., and WINGROVE, J. (1974), *The Handicapped Person in the Community*, Tavistock, London.

BOURDIEU, P., and PASSERON, J. C. (1977), *Reproduction in Education Society and Culture*, Sage, London.

BOWLES, S., and GINTIS, H. (1976), *Schooling in Capitalist America*, Routledge & Kegan Paul, London.

BOWLES, S., and GINTIS, H. (1977), 'I.Q. in the U.S. Class Structure' in J. Karabel and A. H. Halsey (eds), *Power and Ideology in Education*, Oxford University Press.

BOX, S. (1977), 'Hyperactivity – the scandalous silence', *New Society*, 1 December.

BRENNAN, W. K. (1974), *Shaping the Education of Slow Learners*, Routledge & Kegan Paul, London.

BRENNAN, W. K. (1979), *Curricular Needs of Slow Learners*, Schools Council Working Paper No. 63, Evans-Methuen, London.

BRIDGEMAN, T., and FOX, J. (1978), 'Why People Choose Private Schools', *New Society*, 29 June.

BRINDLE, P. (1973), 'The ascertainment of mild subnormality in education', unpublished MEd. dissertation, University of Birmingham.

BRINDLEY, A. (1979), 'A Preparation for Passivity', *Special Education. Forward Trends*, vol. 6, no. 3.

BRITTAN, E. (1976), 'Teacher opinion on aspects of school life – pupils and teachers', *Educational Research*, vol. 18, no. 3.

BROADFOOT, P. (1979), *Assessment in Schools and Society*, Methuen, London.

BURT, C. (1921), *Mental and Scholastic Tests*, Staples Press, London.

BURT, C. (1935), *The Subnormal Mind*, Oxford University Press.

BURT, C. (1937), *The Backward Child*, London University Press.

CASH, J. (1978), 'School Doctors and Warnock', *Special Education. Forward Trends*, vol. 5, no. 3.

CASHMORE, E. (1979), *Rastaman*, Allen & Unwin. London.

Cause for Concern — West Indian Pupils in Redbridge (1978), Black People's Progressive Association and Redbridge Community Relations Council.

CAVE, C., and MADDISON, P. (1978), *A Survey of Recent Research in Special Education*, NFER, Slough.

CHAZAN, M., LAING, A., *et al.* (1980), *Some of our Children — the Early Education of Children with Special Needs*, Open Books, London.

Children and Their Primary Schools. Report of the Central Advisory Council (England) for Education (1967), HMSO, London (the Plowden Report).

CITY OF BIRMINGHAM (1977), *Triennial Report of the Education (Careers Sub-Committee)*, Birmingham Education Authority, March.

CLARK, SIR GEORGE (1964), *A History of the Royal College of Physicians of London*, 2 vols, Clarendon Press, Oxford.

CLEUGH, M. F. (1961), *Teaching the Slow Learners in the Special School*, Methuen, London.

COARD, B. (1971), *How the West Indian Child is Made Educationally Subnormal in the British School System*, New Beacon Books, London.

COLLMAN, R. D. (1956), 'Employment success of ESN-M pupils in England', in *The Slow-Learning Child*, vol. 3, and *American Journal of Mental Deficiency*, vol. 60.

Committee on Defective and Epileptic Children (1898), *Report*, HMSO, London.

COOKSON, C. (1978), 'Courts will decide whether tests are culturally biased', *The Times Educational Supplement*, 20 October.

Court Report, see *Fit for the Future . . .* (1976).

COX, C. B. and BOYSON, R. (1977), *Black Paper 1977*, Temple-Smith, London.

COX, C. B. and DYSON, A. E. (eds) (1969), *Fight for Education — A Black Paper*, Critical Quarterly Society.

CRAFT, M. (ed.) (1970), *Family, Class and Education — A Reader*, Longman, London.

CURTIS, M. (1980), 'Social skills — taught not caught', *Special Education — Forward Trends*, vol. 7, no. 3.

DAVID, M. (1980), *The State, the Family and Education*, Routledge & Kegan Paul, London.

DEPARTMENT OF EDUCATION AND SCIENCE (1965), *Special Education Today*, Report on Education no. 23, HMSO, London.

DEPARTMENT OF EDUCATION AND SCIENCE (1972), *The Health of the School Child, 1969–70 Report*, The chief medical officer to the DES, HMSO, London

DEPARTMENT OF EDUCATION AND SCIENCE (1973), 'Educational arrangements for children who may need special education', letter to chief education officers, November.

DEPARTMENT OF EDUCATION AND SCIENCE (1975a), *The Discovery of Children Requiring Special Education and an Assessment of Their Needs*, Circular 2/75, HMSO, London.

DEPARTMENT OF EDUCATION AND SCIENCE (1975b), *Educating Mentally Handicapped Children*, Education Pamphlet no. 60, HMSO, London.

DEPARTMENT OF EDUCATION AND SCIENCE (1977a),*Education in Schools — A Consultative Document*, Cmnd 6869, HMSO, London.

DEPARTMENT OF EDUCATION AND SCIENCE (1977b), *Review of Forms SE1–SE6*, Circular 14/77, HMSO, London.

DEPARTMENT OF EDUCATION AND SCIENCE (1978), *Behavioural Units — A Survey of Special Units for Pupils with Behavioural Problems*, Information Division, Department of Education and Science, HMSO, London.

DEPARTMENT OF EDUCATION AND SCIENCE (1980a), *A Framework for the School Curriculum — proposals for consultation by the Secretaries of State for Education for England and Wales*, HMSO, London.

DEPARTMENT OF EDUCATION AND SCIENCE (1980b), *Special Needs in Education*, white paper, Cmnd 7996, HMSO, London.

DESCOEUDRES, A. (1928), *The Education of the Mentally Defective Child*, Harrap, London (2nd edn trans. from the French by S. Row).

DEXTER, L. A. (1958), 'A social theory of mental deficiency', *American Journal of Mental Deficiency*, vol. 63.

DHONDY, F. (1974), 'The black explosion in schools', *Race Today*, February.

DOERINGER, R. B., and PIORE, M. J. (1971), *International Labour Markets and Manpower Analysis*, D. C. Heath, Lexington, Mass.

DOWNES, D. (1966), *The Delinquent Solution*, Routledge & Kegan Paul, London.

DUGDALE, D. (1910), *The Jukes — a Study in Crime. Pauperism and Disease*, Putnam, New York.

EDEN, D. J. (1976), *Mental Handicap — An Introduction*, Unwin Educational Books, London.

EDWARDS, V. (1979), *The West Indian Language Issue in British Schools*, Routledge & Kegan Paul, London.

EGERTON COMMISSION, see *Report of the Royal Commission on the Blind . . .* (1889).

EGGLESTON, J. (1977), *The Sociology of the School Curriculum*, Routledge & Kegan Paul, London.

EGGLESTON, J. (1979), Introduction to P. Broadfoot,*Assessment Schools and Society*, Methuen, London.

ESLAND, G. (1976), 'Diagnosis and Therapy', in G. Esland and G. Salaman (eds), *The Politics of Work and Occupation*, Open University Books, Milton Keynes.

ETZIONI, A. (ed.) (1969), *The Semi-Professions and their Organisation*, Free Press, New York.

Fit for the Future. The Report of the Committee on Child Health Services (1976), Cmnd 6684, HMSO (the Court Report).

FLOUD, J., and SCOTT, W. (1961), 'Recruitment to teaching in England and Wales', in A. M. Halsey, J. Floud and C. A. Anderson (eds), *Education, Economy and Society*, Free Press, Macmillan, London.

FORD, J. (1969), *Social Class and the Comprehensive School*, Routledge & Kegan Paul, London.

FRANCIS, M. (1979), 'Disruptive units – labelling a new generation', *New Approaches in Multi-Racial Education*, vol. 8, no. 1.

GALTON, F. (1869), *Hereditary Genuis – an Inquiry into its Laws and Consequences*, Macmillan, London.

GILES, R. (1977), *The West Indian Experience in British Schools*, Heinemann, London.

GODDARD, H. H. (1912), *The Kallikak Family*, Macmillan, New York.

GOODE, W. J. (1957), 'Community within a community – the Professions', *American Sociological Review*, vol. 22.

GRACE, G. (1978), *Teachers, Ideology and Control*, Routledge & Kegan Paul, London.

GULLIFORD, R. (1969), *Backwardness and Educational Failure*, Routledge & Kegan Paul, London.

GULLIFORD, R. (1971), *Special Educational Needs*, Routledge & Kegan Paul, London.

GUNZBERG, H. C. (1977), *Progress Assessment Chart of Social and Personal Development*, ENFA, Stratford-upon-Avon.

HABERMAS, J. (1973), *Legitimation Crisis*, Heinemann, London.

HALSEY, A. H. (1970), introduction to N. Dennis (ed.), *People and Planning – the Sociology of Housing in Sunderland*, London, Faber.

HALSEY, A. H., FLOUD, J., and ANDERSON, C. A. (1961), *Education, Economy and Society*, Free Press, Macmillan, London.

HALSEY, A. H., HEATH, A. F., and RIDGE, J. M. (1980), *Origins and Destinations. Family Class and Education in Modern Britain*. Clarendon Press, Oxford.

HARGREAVES, D. (1967), *Social Relations and the Secondary Modern School*, Routledge & Kegan Paul, London.

HARGREAVES, D. (1972), *Interpersonal Relations in Education*, Routledge & Kegan Paul, London.

HARGREAVES, D. (1979), 'Durkheim, deviance and education', in L. Barton and R. Meighan, *Schools, Pupils and Deviance*, Nafferton Books, Driffield.

HARGREAVES, D. (1980), 'The occupational culture of teachers', in P. Woods (ed.), *Teacher Strategies*, Croom Helm, London.

HARTMANN, P., and HUSBAND, C. (1974), *Racism and the Mass Media*, Davis-Poynter, London.

HEARNSHAW, L. A. (1979), *Cyril Burt – Psychologist*, Hodder & Stoughton, London.

HEGARTY, S. (1980), 'Integration – some questions to ask', *Special Education – Forward Trends*, vol. 7, no. 1.

HEGARTY, S., POCKLINGTON, K., and LUCAS, D. (1981), *The Education of Handicapped Children in Ordinary Schools*, NFER, London.

HODGSON, K. W. (1953), *The Deaf and their Problems*, Watts, London.

HOGHUGI, M. (1980), 'Assessment and treatment in special education – an overview of the problems', National Council for Special Education, annual conference, Middlesbrough, Cleveland.

HUGHES, E. (1965), 'Professions', *Daedalus*, Spring, Houghton-Mifflin, Boston.

HUGHES, E. C. (1971), *The Sociological Eye. Collected Papers*, Aldine, Chicago.

HUNT, S. (1973), *Parents of the ESN*, National Elfrida Rathbone Society, Liverpool.

INNER LONDON EDUCATION AUTHORITY (1968), *The Education of Immigrant Pupils in Special Schools for ESN Children*, Report 657, ILEA, London.

ITARD, J. M. G. (1894), *De L'Education d'un sauvage*, Paris. (*The Wild Boy of Aveyron*, trans. G. and M. Humphrey, New York, 1932.)

JACKSON, J. A. (ed.) (1970), *Professions and Professionalization*, Cambridge University Press.

JACKSON, P. W. (1968), *Life in Classrooms*, Holt, Rinehart & Winston, New York.

JACKSON, R. (1978), 'Are we unrealistic about jobs?' *Special Education – Forward Trends*, vol. 5, no. 1, March.

JAMES, A. (1979), 'The multi-cultural curriculum', *New Approaches in Multi-Racial Education*, vol. 8, no. 1.

JARVIS, F. (1977), Letter to *New Society*, 8 December.

JEFFCOATE, R. (1979), *Positive Image. Towards a Multi-Cultural Curriculum*, Writers' and Readers' Publishing Cooperative and Chameleon Books, London.

JEFREE, D. M., MCCONKEY, R., and HEWSON, S. (1977), *Teaching the Mentally Handicapped Child*, Souvenir Press, London.

JERROLD, M. A., and FOX, R. (1968), 'Pre-jobs for the boys', *Special Education*, vol. 57, no. 2.

JOHNSON, T. J. (1972), *Professions and Power*, Macmillan, London.

JONES, E. (1981), 'A Resource Approach to Meeting Special Needs in a Secondary School', in L. Barton and S. Tomlinson (eds), *Special Education – Policy, Practices and Social Issues*, Harper & Row, London.

KAMIN, L. J. (1977), *The Science and Politics of I. Q.*, Penguin, Harmondsworth.

KARABEL, J., and HALSEY, K. (1977), *Power and Ideology in Education*, Oxford University Press.

KEDDIE, N. (1970), 'Classroom knowledge', in M. F. D. Young (ed.),

Knowledge and Control, Macmillan, London.

KELLMAN, H. (1970), 'The relevance of social research to social issues – problems and pitfalls', *Sociological Review Monograph*, no. 16.

KELLMER-PRINGLE, M., *et al.* (1966), *11,000 Seven Year Olds*, National Children's Bureau, London.

KENNEDY, I. (1980), 'Unmasking medicine' (the first Reith lecture), *The Listener*, 6 November, p. 600.

KING, R. (1978), *All Things Bright and Beautiful*, Open Books, London.

KIRP, D. (1980), 'Opening the door to the gilded cage', *The Times Educational Supplement*, 19 September.

KNIGHT, D. J., and WALKER, M. A. (1965), 'The factory day at school', *Special Education*, vol. 54, no. 3.

KOGAN, M. (1978), *The Politics of Curriculum Change*, Fontana, London.

LACEY, C. (1967), *Hightown Grammar*, Routledge & Kegan Paul, London.

LAING, A. F., CHAZAN, M., *et al.* (1976), *Report of a Research Project on Services for Parents of Handicapped Children*, University College of Swansea, Wales.

LARSON, MAGALI S. (1977), *The Rise of Professionalism – A Sociological Analysis*, University of California Press.

LAWTON, D. (1975), *Class, Culture and the Curriculum*, Routledge & Kegan Paul, London.

LAWTON, D. (1979), *The Politics of the School Curriculum*, Routledge & Kegan Paul, London.

LEEMING, K., SWANN, W., COUPE, J., and MITTLER, P. (1979), *Teaching Language and Communication to the Mentally Handicapped*, Evans, London.

LEWIS, I., and VULLIAMY, G. (1979), 'Where Warnock went wrong', *The Times Educational Supplement*, 30 November.

LINDSEY, M. M. (1957), 'Special schools now and in the future', *Special Schools Journal*, vol. 46, no. 1.

LLOYD-SMITH, M. (1978), 'The meaning of special units', *Socialism and Education*, vol. 6, no. 2.

LOCKWOOD, D. (1973), 'The distribution of power in industrial society', in J. Urry and J. Wakeford (eds), *Power in Britain*, Heinemann, London.

MACMASTER, J. (1973), *Towards a Theory for the Mentally Handicapped*, Edward Arnold, London.

MCNAMARA, D. (1977), 'A time for change. A reappraisal of the sociology of education as a contributing discipline to Professional Education Courses', *Educational Studies*, vol. 3, no. 3.

MEICHENBAUM, D. (1976), 'Cognitive behaviour modification', in J. T. Spence, R. C. Carson, and J. W. Thibaut (eds), *Behaviour Approach to Therapy*, General Learning Press, New Jersey.

MEIGHAN, R. (1981), *The Sociology of Educating*, Holt-Saunders, London.

MINISTRY OF EDUCATION (1945), 'Handicapped Pupils and School Health

Service Regulations', *Statutory rules and orders* no. 1076, HMSO, London.

MINISTRY OF EDUCATION (1946), *Special Educational Treatment*, Pamphlet no. 5, HMSO, London.

MINISTRY OF EDUCATION (1956), *Education of the Handicapped Pupil 1945—55*, Pamphlet no. 3, HMSO, London.

MINISTRY OF EDUCATION (1961), *Special Educational Treatment for ESN Pupils*, Circular 11/61, HMSO, London.

MITTLER, P. (1978), 'Choices in partnership', in *Lebenshife Für Behinderte*, The world congress of the International Society for Mental Handicap on Mental Handicap, ISMH, pp. 242–51.

MORRISON, A., and MCINTYRE, D. (1969), *Teachers and Teaching*, Penguin, Harmondsworth.

MOWAT, C. (1961), *The Charity Organisation Society*, Methuen, London.

MYRDAL, A. (1944), *An American Dilemma*, Harper, New York.

MUSGRAVE, P. W. (1972), 'Social factors affecting the curriculum', in P. W. Hughes (ed.), *The Teacher's Role in Curriculum Design*, Angus & Richardson. London.

NATIONAL ASSOCIATION FOR SPECIAL EDUCATION (1966), 'What is special about special education', *Proceedings of the First International Conference*, Avery Hill, London.

NATIONAL COUNCIL FOR SPECIAL EDUCATION (1979), *Newsletter*, vol. 7.

NATIONAL COUNCIL FOR SPECIAL EDUCATION (1980), *Techniques and Strategies*, 8th Annual Conference, Middlesbrough, Cleveland.

NATIONAL UNION OF TEACHERS (1930), *The Education of Mentally Defective Children – a reply to the Wood Committee*, NUT, London.

NATIONAL UNION OF TEACHERS (1979), *Special Educational Needs* (The NUT reply to the Warnock Report), NUT, London.

NATIONAL UNION OF TEACHERS (Avon) (1980), *After the fire – a report on St Pauls and multi-ethnic education*, Bristol.

NEWELL, P. (1980), 'What are the alternatives?', *Conference Proceedings*, Advisory Centre for Education/National Association for Multi-Racial Education, Conference on Disruptive Units, London, May.

NEWELL, P. (1981), 'The case of the missing provision', *The Times Educational Supplement*, 16 January.

Parents Voice, (1978), Letters, vol. 28, no. 1.

PARSONS, T. (1952), *The Social System*, Free Press, New York.

PHILLIPS, R. (1979), *Education for Racial Domination*, Pan-African Institute, London.

PLOWDEN REPORT, see *Children and their Primary Schools . . .* (1967).

POCKLINGTON, K. (1980), 'Integration – a lesson from America', *Special Education – Forward Trends*, vol. 7, no. 3.

PRESLAND, J., and ROBERTS, G. (1980), 'Aims, objectives and ESN(S) children', *Special Education – Forward Trends*, vol. 7, no. 2.

PRITCHARD, D. G. (1963), *Education of the Handicapped 1760–1960*, Routledge & Kegan Paul, London.

QUIRK COMMITTEE, see *Speech Therapy Services . . .* (1972).

Race Today (1975), 'Who's educating who – the black education movement and the struggle for power', August.

REDBRIDGE STUDY, see, *Cause for Concern*.

Report of the Committee on Maladjusted Children (1955), HMSO, London (the Underwood Committee).

Report of the Mental Deficiency Committee (1929), Board of Education and Board of Control, HMSO, London (the Wood Report).

Report of the Royal Commission on the Blind, the Deaf, the Dumb and Others of the United Kingdom (1889), 4 vols, HMSO, London (the Egerton Commission).

Report of the Royal Commission on the Care and Control of the Feeble-Minded (1908), HMSO, London.

REYNOLDS, D. (1981), 'The comprehensive experience', paper given to 4th Sociology of Education Conference, Westhill College, Birmingham, January.

REYNOLDS, D., and SULLIVAN, M. (1979), 'Bringing schools back in', in L. Barton and R. Meighan (eds), *Schools, Pupils and Deviance*, Nafferton Books, Driffield.

REYNOLDS, J. (1982), *A Dictionary of Education*, Routledge & Kegan Paul, London.

REX, J. (1971), *Race Relations in Sociological Theory*, Weidenfeld & Nicolson, London.

REX, J. (1973), *Discovering Sociology*, Routledge & Kegan Paul, London.

REX, J. (1974), *Sociology and the Demystification of the Modern World*, Routledge & Kegan Paul, London.

REX. J., and TOMLINSON, S. (1979), *Colonial Immigrants in a British City*, Routledge & Kegan Paul, London.

RICHMOND, R. (1979), 'Warnock – Found wanting and waiting', *Special Education – Forward Trends*, vol. 6, no. 3.

ROBINSON, W. (1979), 'How can we involve the parents?', *Special Education – Forward Trends*, vol. 6, no. 2.

ROUSSEAU, J.-J. (1762), *Emile*, Paris.

RUTTER, M., TIZARD, J., and WHITMORE, K. (eds) (1970), *Education Health and Behaviour*, Longman, London.

RUTTER, M., COX, A., TUPLING, C., BERGER, M., AND YULE, W. (1975), 'Attainment and adjustment in two geographical areas – the prevalence of psychiatric disorder', *British Journal of Psychiatry*, vol. 126.

SCOTT, R. (1970), 'The social construction of the conception of stigma by professional experts', in J. Douglas (ed.), *Deviance and Respectability*, Basic Books, New York.

SEGAL, S. (1974), *No Child is Ineducable*, Pergamon Press, Oxford.

SELECT COMMITTEE ON RACE RELATIONS AND IMMIGRATION (1973), *Education*, 3 vols, HMSO, London.

SELECT COMMITTEE ON RACE RELATIONS AND IMMIGRATION (1976–7), *The West Indian Community*, 3 vols, HMSO, London.

SEWELL, G. (1981), 'The Micro-Sociology of Segregation Case Studies in the exclusion of children with special needs from ordinary schools', in L. Barton and S. Tomlinson (eds), *Special Education – Policy, Practices and Social Issues*, Harper & Row, London.

SHARP, R. G., and GREEN, A. (1973), *Education and Social Control*, Routledge & Kegan Paul, London.

SHERIDAN, M. (1965), *The Handicapped Child and his Home*, National Convocation Lecture, London.

SHILS, E. A. (1968), 'The profession of science', *Advancement of Science*, vol. 24.

SKINNER, B. F. (1953), *Science and Human Behaviour*, Macmillan, New York.

SPEAKE, B., and WHELAN, E. (1977), 'Work preparation courses are helping handicapped school leavers find permanent jobs', *Department of Employment Gazette*, vol. 85, no. 8, August.

Special Educational Needs, The Report of the Committee of Enquiry into the Education of Handicapped Children and Young People (1978), HMSO, London (Warnock Report).

SPECTRE, M., and KITSUSE, T. (1977), *Constructing Social Problems*, Cummings, California.

Speech Therapy Services. Report of the Committee appointed by the Secretaries of State (1972), HMSO, London (the Quirk Committee).

SPRAGG, J. (1976), 'The End of an Era' (mimeo), article on the development of Calthorpe School, Birmingham.

SQUIBB, P. (1981), 'A structuralist approach to special education', in L. Barton and S. Tomlinson (eds), *Special Education – Policy, Practices and Social Issues*, Harper & Row, London.

STAPLES, I., and LANE, J. (1980), 'Micro-computers in special education', *Special Education – Forward Trends*, vol. 7, no. 4.

STEIN, Z., and SUSSER, M. (1960), 'Families of dull children, pt. II. Identifying family types and subcultures', *Journal of Mental Science*, vol. 106, no. 445.

STEVENS, M (1976), *The Educational and Social Needs of Children with Severe Handicap* (2nd edn), Edward Arnold, London.

STOTT, D. (1966), *Studies of Troublesome Children*, Tavistock, London.

STRIVENS, J. (1981), 'The use of behaviour modification in special education – a critique', in L. Barton and S. Tomlinson (eds), *Special Education – Policy, Practices and Social Issues*, Harper & Row, London.

STUBBS, M., and DELAMONTE, S. (eds) (1976), *Explorations in Classroom Observation*, Wiley, London.

TANSLEY, A. E., and GULLIFORD, R. (1960), *The Education of Slow-Learning Children*, Routledge & Kegan Paul, London.

TAYLOR, W. (ed.) (1969), *Towards a Policy for the Education of Teachers*, Butterworth, London.

TAYLOR, W., and TAYLOR, I. W. (1970), *Services for the Handicapped in India*, International Society for the Rehabilitation of the Disabled, New York.

TAYLOR REPORT, see *A New Partnership for our Schools* . . . (1977).

THOMAS, M. G. (1957), 'The Royal National Institute for the Blind 1868–1956', *Brighton Herald*.

The Times (1980a), 'Asian Children in Bradford Prone to Greater Handicap', 20 August.

The Times (1980b), 'Drug abuse in control of prisoners – report says' (a comment on the 1980 Report of the Radical Alternatives to Prison Society), 25 October.

The Times (1980c), 'Views being canvassed on testing performance of West Indian children', 30 December.

The Times Educational Supplement (1979), 'Letters', 29 December.

The Times Educational Supplement (1980a), 'Comment', 8 August.

The Times Educational Supplement (1980b), 'Stepping Back From Warnock', 21 November.

TIZARD, J. (1974), *Mental Retardation*, Butterworth, London.

TIZARD, J., and GRAD, J. C. (1961), *The Mentally Handicapped and their Families – a Social Survey*, Oxford University Press.

TOMLINSON, S. (1978), 'West Indian children and ESN-M schooling', *New Community*, vol. 6, no. 3.

TOMLINSON, S. (1980–1), 'The educational performance of ethnic minority children', *New Community*, vol. 8, no. 3.

TOMLINSON, S. (1981), *Educational Subnormality – a Study in Decision-Making*, Routledge & Kegan Paul, London.

TOPLISS, E. (1977), *Provision for the Disabled*, Blackwell, Oxford, and Martin Robertson, London.

TREDGOLD, A. F. (1908), *Mental Deficiency* (1st edn), Ballière Tindall & Cox, London.

TREDGOLD, R. F., and SODDY, K. (1956), *Mental Deficiency* (9th edn of A. E. Tredgold's work), Baillière, Tindall & Cox, London.

UNDERWOOD COMMITTEE, see *Report of the Committee on Maladjusted Children* (1955).

WAKEFORD, J. (1969), *The Cloistered Elite*, Macmillan, London.

WARNOCK, M. (1977), *Schools of Thought*, Faber & Faber, London.

WARNOCK, M. (1979), *Education – a Way Ahead*, Blackwell, Oxford.

WARNOCK, M. (1980a). 'A flexible framework', *The Times Educational Supplement*, 26 September.

WARNOCK, M. (1980b), 'Warnock and the White Paper', *Special Education –*

Forward Trends, vol. 7, no. 4.

WARNOCK REPORT, see *Special Educational Needs* . . . (1978).

WEATHERLEY, R., and LIPSKY, M. (1977), 'Street level bureaucrats and institutional innovation – implementing special education reform', *Harvard Educational Review*, 47(2).

WEBER, M. (1949), *The Methodology of the Social Sciences* (trans. E Shils and H. A. Finch), Free press, Chicago.

WEBER, M. (1972), 'Selections on education and politics', in B. Cosin (ed.), *Education Structure and Society*, Penguin, Harmondsworth.

WERNER-PUTNAM, R. (1979), 'Special education – some cross-national comparisons', *Comparative Education*, vol. 15, no. 1.

WILLIAMS, A. A. (1970), *Basic Subjects for Slow Learners*, Methuen Educational Books, London.

WILLIAMS, P. (1980), 'The deserted garden', lecture given at the 8th National Conference of the National Council for Special Education, Middlesbrough, Cleveland, April 1980. Printed in *Techniques and Strategies*, NCSE, Cleveland.

WILLIAMS, P., and GRUBER, E. (1967), *Response to Special Schooling*, Longman, London.

WILLIS, P. (1977), *Learning to Labour – How Working-Class Boys get Working-Class Jobs*, Saxon House, London.

WILSON, M. (1978), 'Schools – An Evolutionary View', *Special Education – Forward Trends*, vol. 5, no. 3.

WILSON, M. (1980), *Education of Disturbed Pupils*, Schools Council Working Paper 65, Methuen Educational Books, London.

WOOD REPORT, see *Report of the Mental Deficiency Committee* (1929).

WOODS, P. (1979), *The Divided School*, Routledge & Kegan Paul, London.

WOODS, P. (ed.) (1980a), *Pupil Strategies*, Croom Helm, London.

WOODS, P. (ed.) (1980b), *Teacher Strategies*, Croom Helm, London.

WRIGHT MILLS, C. (1951), *White Collar – The American Middle Classes*, Oxford University Press.

WRIGHT MILLS, C. (1959), *The Sociological Imagination*, Oxford University Press.

YOUNG, M. F. D. (1971), *Knowledge and Control*, Collier-Macmillan, London.

YOUNGHUSBAND, E. (1970), *Living with Handicap*, National Children's Bureau, London.

ZETTEL, J. (1978), 'America's new law on Integration', *Special Education – Forward Trends*, vol. 5, no. 2.

Acts of Parliament

1867 Metropolitan Poor Act, Victoria, c. 6
1870 Elementary Education Act, Victoria, c. 75
1876 Elementary Education Act, Victoria, c. 79
1886 Idiots Act, Victoria, c. 25
1891 Lunacy Act, Victoria, c. 65
1893 Elementary Education (Blind and Deaf Children) Act, Victoria, c. 42
1899 Elementary Education (Defective and Epileptic Children) Act, Victoria, c. 32
1903 Elementary Education (Defective and Epileptic Children) Amendment Act, Edward VII, c. 13
1913 Mental Deficiency Act, George V, c. 28
1914 Elementary Education (Defective and Epileptic Children) Act, George V, c. 45
1921 Education Act, George V, c. 51
1927 Mental Deficiency Act, George V, c. 33
1944 Education Act, George VI, c. 31
1946 National Health Service Act, George VI, c. 81
1948 Education (Miscellaneous Provisions) Act, George VI, c. 40
1959 Mental Health Act, Elizabeth II, c. 72
1970 Education (Handicapped Children) Act, Elizabeth II, c. 52
1976 Education Act, Elizabeth II, c. 81
1980 Education Act, Elizabeth II, c. 20
1981 Education Bill, 48, January

Index

Stevens, M., 134
Stott, D.H., 60
Strivens, J., 124
structural-functionalist approach,
    13–16, 67, 107, 178–80
Stubbs, M. and Delamonte, S., 118
Summerfield Report (1968), 34

Tansley, A.E. and Gulliford, R., 134
Taylor, W., 106
Taylor, W. and Taylor, I.W., 15
Taylor Report (1977), 108
teach-pupil interaction, 19–20, 118
teachers: and assessment, 91–2, 96–9,
    103–4; autonomy, 144–8;
    constraints on, 129–30, 132–3; and
    curriculum, 138–40; ideologies,
    119, 120; and integration, 79–80;
    as professionals, 91–2; as
    sociologists, 23;
    training/qualifications, 131–2;
    vested interests, 48, 92, 130
technological development, 12
Thomas, M.G., 37
Tizard, J., 73
Tomlinson, Sally, 10, 11, 23–4, 66, 69,
    73, 88, 95, 96, 111, 115, 145, 156,
    159, 162, 163, 166
Topliss, E., 69
Tredgold, A.F., 7, 14, 32, 33, 40–1, 70,
    71, 141
Trevelyan, Sir Charles, 43

Underwood Report (1955), 34, 51

Vernon Report (1972), 35
vested interests, *see* group interests
voluntary agencies/charitable bodies,
    27–30, 35–45

Warner, Dr, 44
Warnock, Mary, 136
Warnock Report, *Special Educational
    Needs* (1978), 9, 13, 14, 23, 26–7, 28,
    35, 52, 54, 55–7, 62, 64, 67, 71, 73,
    74, 78–9, 90–4, 108, 110, 130,
    131–2, 136, 138, 153, 169
Watson, Thomas, 30
Weatherley, R. and Lipsky, M., 120
Weber, Max, 9, 17, 107, 119
Werner-Putnam, R., 76, 80
White, Misses, 31
Williams, A.A., 134
Williams, P., 139
Williams, P. and Gruber, E., 18
Willis, P., 69, 106, 118
Wilson, Mary, 74
Wood Report (1929), 14, 33, 49, 55, 70,
    113, 142, 145, 149
Woods, P., 19, 106, 107, 118, 126, 127

Young, M.F.D., 135
Younghusband, E., 53

Zettel, J., 12, 77